50 Dutch Recipes for Home

By: Kelly Johnson

Table of Contents

- Stroopwafels (Syrup Waffles)
- Bitterballen (Deep-fried Meatballs)
- Hutspot (Mashed Potatoes, Carrots, and Onions)
- Erwtensoep (Dutch Split Pea Soup)
- Boerenkoolstamppot (Kale Mash)
- Poffertjes (Mini Pancakes)
- Hachee (Dutch Beef Stew)
- Appeltaart (Dutch Apple Pie)
- Rookworst (Smoked Sausage)
- Patat met (Fries with Mayonnaise)
- Speculaas (Spiced Biscuits)
- Kibbeling (Battered and Fried Fish)
- Kroket (Croquette)
- Broodje Kroket (Croquette Sandwich)
- Oliebollen (Dutch Doughnuts)
- Zuurkoolstamppot (Sauerkraut Mash)
- Pepernoten (Spiced Cookies, typically eaten around Sinterklaas)
- Tompouce (Pastry with Cream and Icing)
- Hagelslag (Chocolate Sprinkles on Bread)
- Boterkoek (Butter Cake)
- Witlof met ham en kaas (Chicory with Ham and Cheese)
- Krentenbollen (Currant Buns)
- Goudse Kaas (Gouda Cheese)
- Bossche Bol (Chocolate Cream Puff)
- Slavink (Bacon-wrapped Meatloaf)
- Gevulde Koek (Filled Almond Cookie)
- Kroesjebrij (Fruit Pudding)
- Hangop (Dutch Curd)
- Advocaat (Dutch Eggnog)
- Spekdikken (Thick Pancakes with Bacon)
- Broodje Haring (Herring Sandwich)
- Boterham met Kaas (Cheese Sandwich)
- Droge Worst (Dried Sausage)
- Limburgse Vlaai (Limburg Flan)
- Pannenkoeken (Dutch Pancakes)

- Krentenwegge (Currant Loaf)
- Slavinken (Bacon-wrapped Ground Meat Rolls)
- Kapsalon (Meat, French Fries, and Salad)
- Zeeuwse Bolus (Sweet Pastry)
- Balkenbrij (Sausage made from Pork)
- Arretjescake (Chocolate Biscuit Cake)
- Hagel & Wit (Bread with Hagelslag and Butter)
- Haringsalade (Herring Salad)
- Ossenworst (Raw Beef Sausage)
- Kippensoep (Chicken Soup)
- Vlaflip (Dessert with Custard and Yogurt)
- Boerenjongens (Brandy-infused Raisins)
- Romige Aspergesoep (Creamy Asparagus Soup)
- Oosterse Groentensoep (Oriental Vegetable Soup)
- Babi Pangang (Indonesian-style Pork Dish)

Stroopwafels (Syrup Waffles)

Ingredients:

- 2 cups (250g) all-purpose flour
- 1/2 cup (100g) granulated sugar
- 1/2 cup (113g) unsalted butter, softened
- 1 egg
- 1 teaspoon active dry yeast
- 1/4 cup (60ml) warm milk
- 1/2 teaspoon vanilla extract
- 1/4 teaspoon ground cinnamon
- Pinch of salt
- For the syrup filling:
    - 1 cup (200g) brown sugar
    - 1/2 cup (113g) unsalted butter
    - 1 teaspoon ground cinnamon

Instructions:

1. In a small bowl, dissolve the yeast in the warm milk and let it sit for about 5 minutes until foamy.
2. In a large mixing bowl, combine the flour, sugar, softened butter, egg, vanilla extract, ground cinnamon, and salt. Mix until a dough forms.
3. Pour the yeast mixture into the dough and knead until the dough is smooth and elastic. Cover the bowl with plastic wrap and let it rise in a warm place for about 1 hour, or until doubled in size.
4. While the dough is rising, prepare the syrup filling. In a saucepan, combine the brown sugar, butter, and ground cinnamon. Cook over medium heat, stirring constantly, until the mixture is smooth and bubbly. Remove from heat and set aside to cool slightly.
5. Once the dough has risen, divide it into small balls, about the size of a walnut. Preheat a stroopwafel iron or a regular waffle iron.
6. Place a ball of dough onto the center of the preheated iron and close the lid. Cook for about 1-2 minutes, or until golden brown and crispy. Remove the waffle from the iron and immediately slice it in half horizontally using a sharp knife.

7. Spread a spoonful of the warm syrup filling onto one half of the waffle, then place the other half on top and gently press down to sandwich the syrup between the waffle halves. Repeat with the remaining dough balls and syrup filling.
8. Allow the stroopwafels to cool for a few minutes before serving. Enjoy these delicious Dutch treats with a cup of coffee or tea!

This recipe makes about 10-12 stroopwafels, depending on the size of your waffle iron and the thickness of the waffles. Adjust the amount of syrup filling according to your preference for sweetness.

Bitterballen (Deep-fried Meatballs)

Ingredients:

- 1/4 cup (60g) unsalted butter
- 1/3 cup (40g) all-purpose flour
- 1 cup (240ml) beef or veal broth
- 1 cup (150g) cooked beef or veal, finely chopped or shredded
- 2 tablespoons finely chopped onion
- 1 tablespoon finely chopped parsley
- 1/2 teaspoon salt
- 1/4 teaspoon ground black pepper
- Pinch of nutmeg
- 2 eggs
- 1 cup (120g) fine breadcrumbs
- Vegetable oil, for frying
- Mustard, for serving (optional)

Instructions:

1. In a saucepan, melt the butter over medium heat. Stir in the flour and cook, stirring constantly, for 1-2 minutes to make a roux.
2. Gradually whisk in the beef or veal broth until smooth. Cook, stirring constantly, until the mixture thickens and begins to bubble.
3. Stir in the cooked beef or veal, chopped onion, parsley, salt, pepper, and nutmeg. Cook for another 2-3 minutes, then remove from heat.
4. Transfer the mixture to a shallow dish and spread it out evenly. Cover with plastic wrap, pressing it directly onto the surface of the mixture to prevent a skin from forming. Chill in the refrigerator for at least 2 hours, or until firm.
5. Once the mixture is firm, use a spoon to scoop out small portions and roll them into balls, about 1 inch in diameter.
6. In a shallow bowl, beat the eggs. Place the breadcrumbs in another shallow bowl.
7. Dip each meatball into the beaten egg, then roll it in the breadcrumbs until evenly coated. Place the coated meatballs on a baking sheet lined with parchment paper.
8. In a deep fryer or large, heavy-bottomed pot, heat vegetable oil to 350°F (180°C). Fry the meatballs in batches for 3-4 minutes, or until golden brown and crispy. Use a slotted spoon to transfer them to a paper towel-lined plate to drain.

9. Serve the bitterballen hot, with mustard for dipping if desired. Enjoy these delicious Dutch snacks as appetizers or party treats!

This recipe makes about 20-24 bitterballen, depending on the size of your meatballs. Adjust the seasoning according to your taste preferences, and feel free to customize the filling with different herbs and spices.

Hutspot (Mashed Potatoes, Carrots, and Onions)

Ingredients:

- 1 kg (about 2.2 lbs) potatoes, peeled and diced
- 500 g (about 1.1 lbs) carrots, peeled and sliced
- 2 large onions, peeled and chopped
- Salt, to taste
- Pepper, to taste
- Butter, for mashing
- Milk or cream, for mashing
- Optional: smoked sausage or braised beef, for serving

Instructions:

1. In a large pot, bring salted water to a boil. Add the diced potatoes, sliced carrots, and chopped onions to the pot.
2. Cook the vegetables until they are tender, which typically takes about 20-25 minutes.
3. Once the vegetables are cooked, drain them well and return them to the pot.
4. Mash the potatoes, carrots, and onions together using a potato masher or a fork. Add butter and milk or cream to achieve your desired consistency. Season with salt and pepper to taste.
5. Serve the hutspot hot, either on its own or accompanied by smoked sausage or braised beef.
6. Enjoy this comforting Dutch dish with your favorite condiments, such as mustard or pickles, for extra flavor.

Hutspot is a versatile dish that can be easily customized to suit your preferences. Some variations include adding herbs like parsley or thyme for extra flavor, or topping the dish with crispy fried onions for added texture. However you choose to enjoy it, hutspot is sure to warm your heart and satisfy your appetite.

Erwtensoep (Dutch Split Pea Soup)

Ingredients:

- 500g (about 2 cups) dried split peas
- 1 large onion, chopped
- 2 carrots, diced
- 2 celery stalks, diced
- 2 potatoes, peeled and diced
- 200g (about 7 oz) smoked pork shoulder or bacon, diced
- 1 smoked sausage (rookworst)
- 2 bay leaves
- 1 teaspoon dried thyme
- Salt and pepper, to taste
- Chopped fresh parsley, for garnish
- Rye bread or crusty bread, for serving

Instructions:

1. Rinse the dried split peas under cold water and drain them.
2. In a large pot or Dutch oven, combine the split peas, chopped onion, diced carrots, diced celery, diced potatoes, diced smoked pork shoulder or bacon, bay leaves, and dried thyme.
3. Add enough water to cover the ingredients by about 2 inches. Bring the soup to a boil over medium-high heat, then reduce the heat to low and let it simmer, partially covered, for about 1 to 1.5 hours, stirring occasionally. Skim off any foam that rises to the surface.
4. Once the split peas and vegetables are tender and the soup has thickened, remove the bay leaves and discard them.
5. While the soup is simmering, prepare the smoked sausage according to the package instructions. Once cooked, slice the sausage into rounds.
6. Use an immersion blender or a potato masher to partially blend the soup, leaving some chunks of vegetables intact for texture. If the soup is too thick, you can add more water to reach your desired consistency.
7. Season the soup with salt and pepper to taste. Add the sliced smoked sausage to the soup and let it simmer for an additional 10-15 minutes to allow the flavors to meld together.

8. Serve the erwtensoep hot, garnished with chopped fresh parsley, and accompanied by slices of rye bread or crusty bread.

Erwtensoep is even better the next day, as the flavors have a chance to develop further. Store any leftovers in the refrigerator and reheat gently before serving. Enjoy this comforting Dutch split pea soup as a warming meal during the chilly winter months!

Boerenkoolstamppot (Kale Mash)

Ingredients:

- 1 kg (about 2.2 lbs) potatoes, peeled and cut into chunks
- 500 g (about 1 lb) kale, stems removed and chopped
- 1 large onion, chopped
- 200 g (about 7 oz) smoked sausage (rookworst)
- 100 ml (about 1/2 cup) milk or cream
- 50 g (about 1/4 cup) butter
- Salt and pepper, to taste
- Mustard, for serving (optional)

Instructions:

1. In a large pot, bring salted water to a boil. Add the potatoes to the pot and cook until they are fork-tender, which typically takes about 15-20 minutes.
2. In a separate pot of boiling water, blanch the chopped kale for about 5 minutes, or until it is tender. Drain the kale and set it aside.
3. While the potatoes are cooking, heat a large skillet over medium heat. Add a splash of oil or butter, then sauté the chopped onion until it is soft and translucent.
4. Once the potatoes are cooked, drain them well and return them to the pot. Add the blanched kale to the pot with the potatoes.
5. Use a potato masher or a fork to mash the potatoes and kale together until they are well combined. Add the milk or cream and butter to the pot and continue mashing until the mixture is smooth and creamy. Season with salt and pepper to taste.
6. While the potatoes and kale are mashing, prepare the smoked sausage according to the package instructions. Once cooked, slice the sausage into rounds.
7. Serve the boerenkoolstamppot hot, topped with slices of smoked sausage. If desired, serve with mustard on the side for extra flavor.

Boerenkoolstamppot is a comforting and satisfying meal that's perfect for chilly evenings. It's a great way to enjoy the flavors of kale and potatoes in a hearty and nutritious dish. Enjoy this classic Dutch favorite with your family and friends!

Poffertjes (Mini Pancakes)

Ingredients:

- 250g (about 2 cups) all-purpose flour
- 1 teaspoon instant yeast
- 1 tablespoon granulated sugar
- 1/2 teaspoon salt
- 300ml (about 1 1/4 cups) lukewarm milk
- 2 large eggs
- Butter, for greasing the pan
- Powdered sugar, for serving
- Optional toppings: additional butter, syrup, fruit, whipped cream

Instructions:

1. In a large mixing bowl, whisk together the flour, instant yeast, sugar, and salt.
2. Gradually add the lukewarm milk to the dry ingredients, stirring continuously to form a smooth batter.
3. Beat the eggs in a separate bowl, then add them to the batter and mix until well combined.
4. Cover the bowl with plastic wrap or a clean kitchen towel and let the batter rest at room temperature for about 30 minutes. This allows the yeast to activate and the batter to rise slightly.
5. Heat a poffertjes pan over medium heat and lightly grease the indentations with butter.
6. Fill each indentation of the pan about three-quarters full with batter using a spoon or a squeeze bottle.
7. Cook the poffertjes for about 2-3 minutes, or until small bubbles form on the surface and the bottoms are golden brown.
8. Use a fork or a wooden skewer to carefully flip each poffertje over and cook for an additional 1-2 minutes, or until the other side is golden brown and cooked through.
9. Transfer the cooked poffertjes to a plate and continue cooking the remaining batter in batches, greasing the pan as needed.
10. Serve the poffertjes hot, dusted with powdered sugar and topped with a pat of butter. Enjoy them plain or with your favorite toppings such as syrup, fruit, or whipped cream.

Poffertjes are best enjoyed fresh and warm, so serve them immediately for the ultimate indulgence. They're perfect for breakfast, brunch, or as a sweet snack any time of day!

Hachee (Dutch Beef Stew)

Ingredients:

- 1 kg (about 2.2 lbs) beef chuck or stewing beef, cut into cubes
- 2 large onions, thinly sliced
- 2 tablespoons all-purpose flour
- 2 tablespoons butter or vegetable oil
- 2 cloves garlic, minced
- 2 bay leaves
- 2 whole cloves
- 1 teaspoon dried thyme
- 1 teaspoon dried rosemary
- 2 tablespoons brown sugar
- 2 tablespoons red wine vinegar
- 500 ml (about 2 cups) beef broth
- Salt and pepper, to taste
- Chopped fresh parsley, for garnish (optional)

Instructions:

1. In a large bowl, season the beef cubes with salt and pepper, then toss them with the all-purpose flour until evenly coated.
2. In a large Dutch oven or heavy-bottomed pot, heat the butter or vegetable oil over medium heat. Add the sliced onions and cook, stirring occasionally, until they are soft and caramelized, about 10-15 minutes.
3. Add the minced garlic to the pot and cook for another 1-2 minutes, until fragrant.
4. Push the onions and garlic to the side of the pot and add the floured beef cubes in a single layer. Cook the beef, stirring occasionally, until it is browned on all sides, about 5-7 minutes.
5. Stir in the bay leaves, whole cloves, dried thyme, dried rosemary, brown sugar, and red wine vinegar, coating the beef and onions evenly with the spices.
6. Pour the beef broth into the pot, stirring to deglaze the bottom and scrape up any browned bits.
7. Bring the stew to a simmer, then reduce the heat to low and cover the pot with a lid. Let the hachee simmer gently for 2-3 hours, stirring occasionally, until the

beef is tender and the flavors have melded together. If the stew becomes too thick during cooking, you can add a bit more beef broth or water as needed.
8. Once the beef is tender, taste the hachee and adjust the seasoning with salt and pepper as needed.
9. Serve the hachee hot, garnished with chopped fresh parsley if desired. Enjoy this delicious Dutch beef stew with mashed potatoes or boiled potatoes for a comforting and satisfying meal!

Hachee is even better when made ahead of time and allowed to sit for a few hours or overnight, as the flavors will continue to develop. It also freezes well, so you can make a big batch and enjoy it later.

Appeltaart (Dutch Apple Pie)

Ingredients:

For the crust:

- 250g (about 2 cups) all-purpose flour
- 125g (about 1/2 cup) granulated sugar
- 125g (about 1/2 cup) unsalted butter, cold and cut into cubes
- 1 large egg
- Pinch of salt

For the filling:

- 6 large apples (such as Granny Smith or Golden Delicious), peeled, cored, and sliced
- 50g (about 1/4 cup) granulated sugar
- 1 teaspoon ground cinnamon
- 1/4 teaspoon ground nutmeg
- 1 tablespoon lemon juice
- Zest of 1 lemon

For the crumb topping:

- 50g (about 1/4 cup) all-purpose flour
- 50g (about 1/4 cup) granulated sugar
- 50g (about 1/4 cup) unsalted butter, cold and cut into cubes

Instructions:

1. Preheat your oven to 180°C (350°F). Grease a 9-inch pie dish or springform pan with butter or non-stick cooking spray.
2. To make the crust, in a large mixing bowl, combine the flour, sugar, and salt. Add the cold cubed butter and rub it into the flour mixture with your fingertips until the mixture resembles coarse crumbs.

3. Add the egg to the mixture and knead until a dough forms. Press the dough into the bottom and up the sides of the prepared pie dish, making sure it's evenly distributed. Set aside.
4. For the filling, in a separate bowl, toss the sliced apples with the granulated sugar, ground cinnamon, ground nutmeg, lemon juice, and lemon zest until well combined.
5. Arrange the apple slices in the prepared crust, making sure they are evenly distributed.
6. To make the crumb topping, in a small bowl, combine the flour and sugar. Add the cold cubed butter and rub it into the flour mixture until it forms coarse crumbs.
7. Sprinkle the crumb topping evenly over the apples in the pie crust.
8. Bake the Dutch apple pie in the preheated oven for 50-60 minutes, or until the crust is golden brown and the apples are tender.
9. Once baked, remove the pie from the oven and let it cool slightly before serving.
10. Serve the Dutch apple pie warm or at room temperature, optionally topped with whipped cream or vanilla ice cream.

Enjoy this delicious Dutch apple pie with friends and family! It's the perfect dessert to celebrate any occasion.

Rookworst (Smoked Sausage)

Here's how you can enjoy rookworst:

1. Boiling: Place the sealed rookworst in a pot of simmering water. Let it cook for about 15-20 minutes, or until heated through. Be careful not to boil the sausage vigorously, as this can cause it to burst.
2. Grilling or Pan-frying: If you prefer a crispier texture, you can grill or pan-fry the rookworst. Simply remove it from the packaging and grill or fry it over medium heat until browned on all sides, about 5-7 minutes per side.
3. Serving: Rookworst can be served in various ways. It's often enjoyed alongside traditional Dutch dishes like stamppot (mashed potatoes mixed with vegetables), hutspot (mashed potatoes, carrots, and onions), or boerenkool (mashed potatoes with kale). You can also slice rookworst and add it to soups, stews, or pasta dishes for added flavor.
4. Condiments: Rookworst pairs well with a variety of condiments. Mustard is a classic choice and adds a tangy kick to the rich sausage flavor. You can also serve it with ketchup, pickles, or sauerkraut for a delicious combination of flavors.

Whether you enjoy it as part of a traditional Dutch meal or incorporate it into your own recipes, rookworst is sure to delight your taste buds with its smoky, savory goodness.

Patat met (Fries with Mayonnaise)

Ingredients:

- Potatoes (enough to make fries for your desired serving size)
- Vegetable oil, for frying
- Salt, to taste
- Mayonnaise, for serving

Instructions:

1. Prepare the potatoes: Start by peeling the potatoes and cutting them into thick strips to resemble French fries.
2. Rinse and dry: Rinse the potato strips under cold water to remove excess starch. Then, pat them dry with a clean kitchen towel or paper towels to ensure they fry up crispy.
3. Preheat the oil: Heat vegetable oil in a deep fryer or large pot to around 350°F (175°C). You want enough oil to submerge the fries completely.
4. Fry the potatoes: Carefully add the potato strips to the hot oil in batches, making sure not to overcrowd the fryer or pot. Fry them for about 4-5 minutes, or until they are golden brown and crispy. Remove the fries from the oil using a slotted spoon and transfer them to a plate lined with paper towels to drain any excess oil. Repeat the frying process with the remaining batches of potatoes.
5. Season with salt: While the fries are still hot, sprinkle them with salt to taste. Toss them gently to ensure the salt is evenly distributed.
6. Serve with mayonnaise: Place the crispy fries on a serving platter or in individual serving cones. Serve them immediately with a generous dollop of mayonnaise on the side for dipping.

Enjoy patat met as a delicious snack or side dish! The combination of crispy fries and creamy mayonnaise is sure to satisfy your cravings for a savory treat reminiscent of Dutch street food culture.

Speculaas (Spiced Biscuits)

Ingredients:

- 250g (about 2 cups) all-purpose flour
- 150g (about 3/4 cup) unsalted butter, softened
- 150g (about 3/4 cup) brown sugar
- 1 egg
- 1 teaspoon baking powder
- 1 teaspoon ground cinnamon
- 1/2 teaspoon ground nutmeg
- 1/4 teaspoon ground cloves
- 1/4 teaspoon ground ginger
- 1/4 teaspoon ground cardamom
- Pinch of salt
- Sliced almonds or whole almonds, for decoration (optional)

Instructions:

1. In a mixing bowl, cream together the softened butter and brown sugar until light and fluffy.
2. Add the egg to the butter-sugar mixture and beat until well combined.
3. In a separate bowl, sift together the flour, baking powder, ground cinnamon, ground nutmeg, ground cloves, ground ginger, ground cardamom, and salt.
4. Gradually add the dry ingredients to the wet ingredients, mixing until a dough forms. If the dough is too sticky, you can add a little more flour as needed.
5. Wrap the dough in plastic wrap and refrigerate it for at least 1 hour, or until firm.
6. Preheat your oven to 180°C (350°F) and line a baking sheet with parchment paper.
7. On a lightly floured surface, roll out the chilled dough to a thickness of about 1/4 inch. Use cookie cutters or wooden molds to cut out shapes from the dough.
8. Transfer the shaped cookies to the prepared baking sheet, leaving some space between each cookie.
9. If desired, press sliced almonds or whole almonds into the tops of the cookies for decoration.
10. Bake the speculaas cookies in the preheated oven for 10-12 minutes, or until the edges are lightly golden brown.

11. Remove the cookies from the oven and let them cool on the baking sheet for a few minutes before transferring them to a wire rack to cool completely.
12. Once cooled, store the speculaas cookies in an airtight container at room temperature. They will keep well for several days.

Enjoy these delicious Dutch spiced cookies with a cup of tea or coffee for a delightful treat that's bursting with flavor!

Kibbeling (Battered and Fried Fish)

Ingredients:

- 500g (about 1 lb) white fish fillets (such as cod, haddock, or pollock), cut into bite-sized pieces
- 150g (about 1 1/4 cups) all-purpose flour
- 1 teaspoon baking powder
- 1/2 teaspoon salt
- 1/4 teaspoon ground black pepper
- 1/4 teaspoon paprika (optional, for extra flavor)
- 200ml (about 3/4 cup) cold beer (such as lager or pilsner)
- Vegetable oil, for frying
- Lemon wedges, for serving (optional)
- Tartar sauce or mayonnaise, for dipping

Instructions:

1. In a large mixing bowl, whisk together the all-purpose flour, baking powder, salt, black pepper, and paprika (if using).
2. Gradually pour in the cold beer, whisking continuously, until you have a smooth batter with the consistency of pancake batter. The batter should be thick enough to coat the back of a spoon but still pourable.
3. Heat vegetable oil in a deep fryer or large pot to 180°C (350°F).
4. Dip the fish pieces into the batter, making sure they are evenly coated on all sides.
5. Carefully lower the battered fish pieces into the hot oil, in batches to avoid overcrowding the fryer. Fry the fish for about 4-5 minutes, or until golden brown and crispy. Use a slotted spoon to remove the fried fish from the oil and transfer them to a plate lined with paper towels to drain any excess oil.
6. Repeat the frying process with the remaining batches of fish.
7. Once all the fish pieces are fried, transfer them to a serving platter. Serve the kibbeling hot, with lemon wedges on the side for squeezing over the fish, and tartar sauce or mayonnaise for dipping.

Enjoy this homemade kibbeling as a delicious snack or appetizer, perfect for sharing with friends and family!

Kroket (Croquette)

Ingredients:

For the filling:

- 250g (about 9 oz) cooked beef, finely shredded or minced
- 2 tablespoons butter
- 3 tablespoons all-purpose flour
- 250ml (about 1 cup) beef broth
- 1 small onion, finely chopped
- 1 clove garlic, minced
- Salt and pepper, to taste
- Pinch of nutmeg (optional)
- Fresh parsley, chopped (optional)

For the breading:

- 2 large eggs
- 100g (about 1 cup) breadcrumbs
- Vegetable oil, for frying

Instructions:

1. Prepare the filling:
   - In a saucepan, melt the butter over medium heat. Add the chopped onion and minced garlic and cook until softened.
   - Stir in the flour to make a roux and cook for a minute or two until golden.
   - Gradually whisk in the beef broth, stirring constantly to prevent lumps from forming.
   - Add the cooked beef to the saucepan and simmer for a few minutes until the mixture thickens.
   - Season with salt, pepper, and a pinch of nutmeg if desired. Stir in chopped parsley if using.
   - Remove the filling from the heat and let it cool completely.
2. Shape the kroketten:

- Once the filling is cooled, shape it into cylindrical croquettes, about 3-4 inches long and 1 inch in diameter. You can use your hands or a spoon to shape them.
- Place the shaped croquettes on a baking sheet lined with parchment paper and refrigerate them for at least 1 hour to firm up.

3. Bread the kroketten:
   - In a shallow bowl, beat the eggs.
   - Place the breadcrumbs in another shallow bowl.
   - Dip each chilled croquette into the beaten eggs, then coat it evenly with breadcrumbs, pressing gently to adhere.

4. Fry the kroketten:
   - Heat vegetable oil in a deep fryer or heavy-bottomed pot to 180°C (350°F).
   - Carefully lower the breaded croquettes into the hot oil in batches, frying for about 3-4 minutes until golden brown and crispy.
   - Use a slotted spoon to remove the fried kroketten from the oil and transfer them to a plate lined with paper towels to drain any excess oil.

5. Serve:
   - Serve the kroketten hot, with mustard or a dipping sauce of your choice.

Enjoy these homemade Dutch kroketten as a delicious snack or appetizer, perfect for any occasion! You can also experiment with different fillings such as chicken, shrimp, or vegetables to create a variety of croquette flavors.

Broodje Kroket (Croquette Sandwich)

Ingredients:

- Kroketten (croquettes) - homemade or store-bought
- Soft bread rolls (such as buns or brioche rolls)
- Mustard or mayonnaise, for serving
- Optional toppings: lettuce, sliced tomato, pickles

Instructions:

1. Prepare the kroketten: If using store-bought kroketten, follow the instructions on the packaging to cook them until they are crispy and golden brown. If making homemade kroketten, follow the recipe provided earlier to prepare and fry them until they are cooked through and crispy.
2. Prepare the bread rolls: Slice the bread rolls in half horizontally, but leave one side intact so that the roll opens like a book.
3. Assemble the sandwiches: Place a cooked kroket on the bottom half of each bread roll. If desired, spread a layer of mustard or mayonnaise on the top half of the roll.
4. Add toppings: For added flavor and texture, you can add optional toppings such as lettuce, sliced tomato, or pickles on top of the kroket.
5. Close the sandwiches: Gently press the top half of each bread roll down onto the kroket and toppings to close the sandwiches.
6. Serve: Serve the broodje kroket sandwiches immediately while the kroket is still hot and crispy. They are best enjoyed fresh, but you can also wrap them in parchment paper or foil to take them on the go.

Broodje kroket is a delicious and comforting snack that's perfect for lunchtime or anytime you're craving something savory and satisfying. Enjoy these Dutch croquette sandwiches with your favorite toppings and condiments for a tasty treat that's sure to please!

Oliebollen (Dutch Doughnuts)

Ingredients:

- 500g (about 4 cups) all-purpose flour
- 7g (about 2 1/4 teaspoons) instant yeast
- 1 teaspoon salt
- 1 tablespoon granulated sugar
- 300ml (about 1 1/4 cups) lukewarm milk
- 2 large eggs, beaten
- 100g (about 1/2 cup) raisins
- 100g (about 1/2 cup) currants
- Optional: chopped apples, citrus zest, or other dried fruits
- Vegetable oil, for frying
- Powdered sugar, for dusting

Instructions:

1. Prepare the dough:
    - In a large mixing bowl, combine the flour, instant yeast, salt, and granulated sugar.
    - Gradually add the lukewarm milk and beaten eggs to the dry ingredients, mixing until a sticky dough forms.
    - Stir in the raisins, currants, and any optional additions such as chopped apples or citrus zest.
2. Let the dough rise:
    - Cover the bowl with plastic wrap or a clean kitchen towel and let the dough rise in a warm, draft-free place for about 1 to 1.5 hours, or until it has doubled in size.
3. Heat the oil:
    - In a deep fryer or large pot, heat vegetable oil to 180°C (350°F).
4. Form and fry the oliebollen:
    - Using two spoons or a cookie scoop, carefully drop spoonfuls of dough into the hot oil, working in batches to avoid overcrowding the fryer.
    - Fry the oliebollen for about 3-4 minutes per side, or until they are golden brown and cooked through. Use a slotted spoon to turn them halfway through cooking.

- Remove the fried oliebollen from the oil and transfer them to a plate lined with paper towels to drain any excess oil. Repeat the frying process with the remaining dough.
5. Serve:
    - Dust the warm oliebollen generously with powdered sugar just before serving.
    - Enjoy the oliebollen hot and fresh, preferably on the same day they are made for the best flavor and texture.

Oliebollen are a delightful indulgence that's perfect for celebrating special occasions or simply enjoying as a sweet treat with family and friends. Serve them alongside a cup of coffee, tea, or hot chocolate for a cozy and festive experience!

Zuurkoolstamppot (Sauerkraut Mash)

Ingredients:

- 1 kg (about 2.2 lbs) potatoes, peeled and cut into chunks
- 500g (about 1 lb) sauerkraut, drained and rinsed
- 200g (about 7 oz) smoked sausage or bacon, diced (optional)
- 1 large onion, chopped
- 2 tablespoons butter
- 100ml (about 1/2 cup) milk or cream
- Salt and pepper, to taste
- Chopped fresh parsley, for garnish (optional)

Instructions:

1. Boil the potatoes: Place the potato chunks in a large pot and cover them with water. Add a pinch of salt to the water and bring it to a boil. Cook the potatoes until they are tender, about 15-20 minutes.
2. Cook the sauerkraut: While the potatoes are boiling, heat a separate pot over medium heat. Add the chopped onion and cook until it's softened and translucent. Add the sauerkraut to the pot and cook it with the onion for a few minutes, stirring occasionally. This will help mellow the flavor of the sauerkraut.
3. Prepare the smoked sausage or bacon: If using smoked sausage or bacon, cook it in a separate pan according to package instructions until it's browned and cooked through. Set aside.
4. Mash the potatoes: Once the potatoes are tender, drain them well and return them to the pot. Add the butter and milk or cream to the pot and mash the potatoes until they are smooth and creamy. Season with salt and pepper to taste.
5. Combine the ingredients: Add the cooked sauerkraut and onion mixture to the mashed potatoes and stir until well combined. If using, add the cooked smoked sausage or bacon to the mixture and stir again.
6. Serve: Transfer the zuurkoolstamppot to a serving dish and garnish with chopped fresh parsley if desired. Serve hot, accompanied by additional smoked sausage or bacon if desired.

Zuurkoolstamppot is a delicious and satisfying dish that's perfect for a cozy dinner on a chilly evening. Enjoy its hearty flavors and comforting warmth with your family and friends!

Pepernoten (Spiced Cookies, typically eaten around Sinterklaas)

Ingredients:

- 200g (about 1 1/2 cups) all-purpose flour
- 100g (about 1/2 cup) brown sugar
- 1 teaspoon baking powder
- 1/2 teaspoon ground cinnamon
- 1/4 teaspoon ground nutmeg
- 1/4 teaspoon ground cloves
- 1/4 teaspoon ground ginger
- Pinch of salt
- 100g (about 1/2 cup) unsalted butter, softened
- 1-2 tablespoons milk
- Optional: additional spices such as cardamom or white pepper, to taste

Instructions:

1. Preheat the oven: Preheat your oven to 160°C (320°F). Line a baking sheet with parchment paper or a silicone baking mat.
2. Prepare the dough: In a large mixing bowl, combine the flour, brown sugar, baking powder, ground cinnamon, ground nutmeg, ground cloves, ground ginger, and a pinch of salt. If desired, you can add additional spices such as cardamom or white pepper for extra flavor.
3. Add the butter: Cut the softened butter into small pieces and add it to the dry ingredients. Use your fingertips to rub the butter into the flour mixture until it resembles coarse crumbs.
4. Form the dough: Gradually add 1-2 tablespoons of milk to the mixture, a little at a time, until a firm dough forms. Use your hands to knead the dough until it comes together into a smooth ball.
5. Shape the cookies: Pinch off small pieces of dough and roll them into small balls, about 1-2 centimeters (1/2 - 3/4 inch) in diameter. Place the balls of dough onto the prepared baking sheet, leaving a little space between each one.
6. Bake the pepernoten: Transfer the baking sheet to the preheated oven and bake the pepernoten for 12-15 minutes, or until they are lightly golden brown and firm to the touch.

7. Cool and store: Remove the pepernoten from the oven and allow them to cool completely on the baking sheet. Once cooled, store the cookies in an airtight container at room temperature.
8. Serve and enjoy: Serve the pepernoten as a festive snack or treat during the Sinterklaas season. They are perfect for sharing with family and friends, and they also make great edible gifts!

Enjoy these homemade pepernoten as a delicious and festive addition to your Sinterklaas celebrations!

Tompouce (Pastry with Cream and Icing)

Ingredients:

For the pastry cream (banketbakkersroom):

- 500ml (about 2 cups) milk
- 100g (about 1/2 cup) granulated sugar
- 4 large egg yolks
- 40g (about 1/3 cup) cornstarch
- 1 teaspoon vanilla extract

For the pastry:

- 1 sheet of puff pastry, thawed if frozen
- Granulated sugar, for sprinkling
- Pink or orange icing (you can use powdered sugar mixed with a little water or lemon juice, tinted with food coloring)

Instructions:

1. Prepare the pastry cream (banketbakkersroom):
    - In a saucepan, heat the milk over medium heat until it begins to steam. Do not let it boil.
    - In a separate bowl, whisk together the granulated sugar, egg yolks, and cornstarch until well combined and smooth.
    - Gradually pour the warm milk into the egg mixture, whisking constantly to prevent curdling.
    - Return the mixture to the saucepan and cook over medium heat, stirring constantly with a wooden spoon, until it thickens and comes to a gentle boil.
    - Remove the pastry cream from the heat and stir in the vanilla extract. Transfer it to a bowl and cover the surface with plastic wrap to prevent a skin from forming. Let it cool completely in the refrigerator.
2. Prepare the puff pastry:

- Preheat your oven to the temperature indicated on the puff pastry package instructions.
- Roll out the puff pastry sheet on a lightly floured surface to a thickness of about 1/4 inch. Trim the edges to form a rectangle.
- Transfer the pastry to a parchment-lined baking sheet and prick the surface all over with a fork. Sprinkle evenly with granulated sugar.
- Bake the pastry in the preheated oven according to the package instructions, or until it is golden brown and puffed up. Let it cool completely.

3. Assemble the tompouce:
   - Once the pastry and pastry cream have cooled, carefully slice the puff pastry horizontally into two equal layers.
   - Spread a thick layer of pastry cream evenly over the bottom pastry layer.
   - Gently place the second pastry layer on top of the pastry cream, pressing down lightly to adhere.
   - Spread the pink or orange icing over the top pastry layer, allowing it to drip down the sides.
   - Refrigerate the tompouce for at least 1 hour to allow the icing to set and the flavors to meld together.

4. Serve and enjoy:
   - Once chilled, use a sharp knife to slice the tompouce into individual portions.
   - Serve the tompouce cold and enjoy its creamy, flaky goodness!

Tompouce is a delightful treat that's sure to impress your family and friends. Enjoy it as a special dessert for any occasion or celebration!

Hagelslag (Chocolate Sprinkles on Bread)

Ingredients:

- Sliced bread of your choice
- Butter or margarine, softened
- Hagelslag (chocolate sprinkles)

Instructions:

1. Toast the bread (optional): If desired, toast the bread slices until they are golden brown and crisp. This step is optional and depends on personal preference.
2. Spread the butter: Spread a generous layer of softened butter or margarine evenly onto each slice of bread. The butter adds richness and helps the hagelslag stick to the bread.
3. Add the hagelslag: Sprinkle a generous amount of hagelslag evenly over the buttered bread slices. You can use as much or as little hagelslag as you like, depending on your taste preferences.
4. Enjoy: Once the hagelslag is added, your chocolate sprinkle bread is ready to be enjoyed! Serve it as a delicious and indulgent breakfast, snack, or treat any time of the day.

Hagelslag on bread is a simple yet delightful treat that's perfect for satisfying your chocolate cravings in the morning or throughout the day. Experiment with different types of bread and hagelslag flavors to find your favorite combination!

Boterkoek (Butter Cake)

Ingredients:

- 250g (about 1 cup) unsalted butter, softened
- 200g (about 1 cup) granulated sugar
- 1 large egg
- 275g (about 2 cups) all-purpose flour
- 1/2 teaspoon baking powder
- Pinch of salt
- Optional: 1 teaspoon almond extract or vanilla extract
- Optional: sliced almonds or coarse sugar for topping

Instructions:

1. Preheat the oven: Preheat your oven to 175°C (350°F). Grease a 9-inch round cake pan or tart pan with butter or non-stick cooking spray, and line the bottom with parchment paper for easy removal.
2. Cream the butter and sugar: In a large mixing bowl, cream together the softened butter and granulated sugar until light and fluffy, using a hand mixer or stand mixer.
3. Add the egg and flavoring: Add the egg to the butter-sugar mixture and beat until well combined. If using almond extract or vanilla extract, add it at this stage and mix until incorporated.
4. Combine the dry ingredients: In a separate bowl, sift together the all-purpose flour, baking powder, and salt.
5. Mix the batter: Gradually add the dry ingredients to the wet ingredients, mixing until a smooth dough forms. Be careful not to overmix.
6. Transfer to the pan: Transfer the dough to the prepared cake pan and use your hands or a spatula to spread it evenly into the pan, pressing down lightly to compact it.
7. Optional topping: If desired, sprinkle sliced almonds or coarse sugar over the top of the dough for added texture and flavor.
8. Bake: Place the cake pan in the preheated oven and bake for 25-30 minutes, or until the boterkoek is golden brown around the edges and set in the center.
9. Cool and slice: Remove the boterkoek from the oven and let it cool in the pan for about 10 minutes before transferring it to a wire rack to cool completely. Once cooled, slice the boterkoek into wedges or squares and serve.

10. Enjoy: Serve the boterkoek slices at room temperature with a cup of coffee or tea for a delightful treat!

Boterkoek is best enjoyed fresh but can be stored in an airtight container at room temperature for up to several days. It's a deliciously simple and satisfying dessert that's sure to become a favorite in your household!

Witlof met ham en kaas (Chicory with Ham and Cheese)

Ingredients:

- 4 to 6 witlof (chicory) heads
- 4 to 6 slices of ham
- 150g (about 1 1/2 cups) grated cheese (Gouda or Emmental work well)
- 30g (about 2 tablespoons) butter
- 30g (about 1/4 cup) all-purpose flour
- 300ml (about 1 1/4 cups) milk
- Salt and pepper, to taste
- Pinch of nutmeg (optional)

Instructions:

1. Prepare the witlof: Trim the base of each witlof head and remove any wilted outer leaves. Cut a shallow "V" shape into the base to remove the bitter core.
2. Steam the witlof: Place the prepared witlof in a steamer basket or pot fitted with a steaming rack. Steam the witlof for about 15 minutes, or until it is tender when pierced with a fork. Remove from the steamer and let it cool slightly.
3. Wrap the witlof in ham: Preheat your oven to 180°C (350°F). Wrap each steamed witlof head with a slice of ham.
4. Prepare the cheese sauce: In a saucepan, melt the butter over medium heat. Once melted, add the flour and stir to form a roux. Cook the roux for 1-2 minutes, stirring constantly, until it becomes fragrant but not browned. Gradually whisk in the milk until smooth. Cook the sauce, stirring constantly, until it thickens and comes to a simmer. Remove from heat and stir in the grated cheese until melted and smooth. Season with salt, pepper, and a pinch of nutmeg, if desired.
5. Assemble the dish: Place the ham-wrapped witlof in a baking dish. Pour the cheese sauce over the top, ensuring each witlof head is evenly coated.
6. Bake: Place the baking dish in the preheated oven and bake for about 15-20 minutes, or until the cheese is melted and bubbly and the ham is slightly crispy around the edges.
7. Serve: Remove from the oven and let it cool slightly before serving. Serve the witlof met ham en kaas hot as a delicious and comforting main dish.

Enjoy this classic Dutch dish of witlof met ham en kaas with your favorite side dishes for a satisfying and flavorful meal!

Krentenbollen (Currant Buns)

Ingredients:

- 500g (about 4 cups) bread flour
- 7g (about 2 1/4 teaspoons) instant yeast
- 50g (about 1/4 cup) granulated sugar
- 1 teaspoon salt
- 300ml (about 1 1/4 cups) lukewarm milk
- 1 large egg
- 75g (about 1/3 cup) unsalted butter, softened
- 200g (about 1 1/4 cups) currants
- Optional: 1 teaspoon ground cinnamon or mixed spice for extra flavor

Instructions:

1. Activate the yeast: In a small bowl, mix the lukewarm milk with a teaspoon of sugar. Sprinkle the yeast over the milk mixture and let it sit for about 5-10 minutes, or until foamy.
2. Prepare the dough: In a large mixing bowl, combine the bread flour, remaining sugar, and salt. Add the softened butter, beaten egg, activated yeast mixture, and optional ground cinnamon or mixed spice. Mix until a rough dough forms.
3. Knead the dough: Turn the dough out onto a lightly floured surface and knead it for about 10 minutes, or until it becomes smooth and elastic. Alternatively, you can use a stand mixer fitted with a dough hook attachment.
4. Incorporate the currants: Flatten the dough slightly and sprinkle the currants over the surface. Fold the dough over the currants and continue kneading until the currants are evenly distributed throughout the dough.
5. First rise: Place the dough in a lightly oiled bowl, cover it with a clean kitchen towel or plastic wrap, and let it rise in a warm, draft-free place for about 1-2 hours, or until it doubles in size.
6. Shape the buns: Once the dough has risen, punch it down to release any air bubbles. Divide the dough into equal-sized portions and shape each portion into a smooth ball. Place the balls on a parchment-lined baking sheet, leaving some space between each bun.
7. Second rise: Cover the baking sheet with a clean kitchen towel or plastic wrap and let the buns rise for another 30-45 minutes, or until they have doubled in size.

8. Bake: Preheat your oven to 190°C (375°F). Bake the krentenbollen in the preheated oven for 15-20 minutes, or until they are golden brown and sound hollow when tapped on the bottom.
9. Cool and serve: Remove the buns from the oven and let them cool on a wire rack. Once cooled, serve the krentenbollen plain or with a layer of butter, and enjoy!

These homemade krentenbollen are sure to be a hit with your family and friends. Enjoy them for breakfast, brunch, or as a delicious snack any time of the day!

Goudse Kaas (Gouda Cheese)

Ingredients:

- Fresh cow's milk
- Cheese culture (mesophilic or thermophilic)
- Rennet
- Cheese salt
- Optional: annatto (for coloring)

Instructions:

1. Heat the milk: Begin by heating the fresh cow's milk to the appropriate temperature, typically around 86°F (30°C) for adding the culture.
2. Add the culture: Once the milk reaches the desired temperature, add the cheese culture and allow it to ripen the milk. This helps develop the flavor and acidity of the cheese.
3. Coagulate the milk: Add the rennet to the milk and gently stir to distribute it evenly. Let the milk sit undisturbed for about 30-60 minutes, or until a clean break is achieved.
4. Cut the curds: Once the milk has coagulated, use a long knife to cut the curds into small pieces. This allows the whey to separate from the curds.
5. Cook the curds: Gradually increase the temperature of the curds while stirring gently. This helps expel more whey from the curds and develops the desired texture of the cheese.
6. Drain the whey: Once the curds have reached the desired firmness, remove them from the heat and allow them to settle. Drain off the whey using a cheesecloth-lined colander or cheese mold.
7. Press the curds: Transfer the drained curds to a cheese mold and press them to expel any remaining whey and shape the cheese. This can be done using a cheese press or by applying weights gradually over time.
8. Age the cheese: After pressing, the cheese is typically brined to add flavor and preserve it. It is then transferred to a cheese cave or aging room to age for a specific period, ranging from a few weeks to several years, depending on the desired flavor and texture.
9. Wax or vacuum seal (optional): Once the cheese has reached the desired age, it can be waxed or vacuum-sealed to prevent mold growth and preserve its flavor and texture.

10. Enjoy: Once properly aged, your homemade Gouda cheese is ready to be enjoyed! Slice it, shred it, or melt it as desired for use in various recipes or enjoy it on its own as a delicious cheese.

Making Gouda cheese at home requires precision and attention to detail, so it's essential to follow a trusted recipe and cheese-making guidelines to achieve the best results. Additionally, proper sanitation practices and cheese-making equipment are crucial to ensure the safety and quality of the finished cheese.

Bossche Bol (Chocolate Cream Puff)

Ingredients:

For the choux pastry:

- 1/2 cup water
- 1/4 cup unsalted butter
- 1/4 teaspoon salt
- 1/2 cup all-purpose flour
- 2 large eggs

For the filling:

- 1 cup heavy cream
- 2 tablespoons powdered sugar
- 1 teaspoon vanilla extract

For the chocolate ganache:

- 4 ounces dark chocolate, chopped
- 1/2 cup heavy cream

Instructions:

1. Preheat the oven: Preheat your oven to 400°F (200°C). Line a baking sheet with parchment paper.
2. Make the choux pastry: In a saucepan, combine water, butter, and salt. Bring to a boil over medium heat. Add flour all at once and stir vigorously until the mixture forms a smooth dough and pulls away from the sides of the pan, about 1-2 minutes. Remove from heat and let it cool slightly.
3. Add eggs: Gradually add eggs to the dough, one at a time, mixing well after each addition until the dough is smooth and glossy.

4. Pipe the pastry: Transfer the choux pastry dough to a piping bag fitted with a large round tip. Pipe small mounds onto the prepared baking sheet, leaving space between each mound.
5. Bake: Place the baking sheet in the preheated oven and bake for 20-25 minutes or until the pastries are puffed and golden brown. Remove from the oven and let them cool completely on a wire rack.
6. Make the filling: In a mixing bowl, whip the heavy cream with powdered sugar and vanilla extract until stiff peaks form.
7. Fill the pastries: Once the pastries are cooled, cut them in half horizontally. Pipe or spoon the whipped cream onto the bottom halves of the pastries. Place the top halves back on.
8. Make the ganache: In a heatproof bowl, combine chopped dark chocolate and heavy cream. Microwave in 30-second intervals, stirring in between, until the chocolate is melted and the mixture is smooth.
9. Coat the pastries: Dip the filled pastries into the chocolate ganache, coating the top completely. Place them on a wire rack to let the ganache set.
10. Serve: Once the ganache has set, your Bossche Bolletjes are ready to be enjoyed! Serve them as a delicious dessert or snack.

These homemade Bossche Bolletjes are sure to impress with their creamy filling and rich chocolate coating. Enjoy the indulgent flavors of this Dutch pastry at home!

Slavink (Bacon-wrapped Meatloaf)

Ingredients:

- 500g (about 1 lb) ground meat (typically a mixture of pork and beef)
- Salt and pepper, to taste
- 1 tablespoon Dijon mustard
- 1 small onion, finely chopped
- 1 clove garlic, minced
- 1 egg
- 8 slices of bacon

Instructions:

1. Preheat the oven: Preheat your oven to 180°C (350°F).
2. Prepare the meat mixture: In a mixing bowl, combine the ground meat, salt, pepper, Dijon mustard, finely chopped onion, minced garlic, and egg. Use your hands or a spoon to mix everything together until well combined.
3. Shape the slavink: Divide the meat mixture into equal portions and shape each portion into a small log or sausage shape, about 8-10cm (3-4 inches) long and 2-3cm (1 inch) thick.
4. Wrap with bacon: Take a slice of bacon and wrap it around each meatloaf, ensuring that the bacon covers the entire surface and overlaps slightly. Secure the ends of the bacon with toothpicks if necessary to prevent them from unraveling during cooking.
5. Cook the slavink: Heat a non-stick skillet over medium heat. Once hot, add the slavink to the skillet and cook for about 2-3 minutes on each side, or until the bacon is lightly browned and crispy.
6. Transfer to the oven: Once the bacon is browned, transfer the slavink to a baking dish or oven-safe skillet. Place it in the preheated oven and bake for an additional 15-20 minutes, or until the meatloaf is cooked through and reaches an internal temperature of at least 70°C (160°F).
7. Serve: Once cooked, remove the slavink from the oven and let it rest for a few minutes before serving. Serve the slavink hot as a main dish with your favorite side dishes, such as mashed potatoes, steamed vegetables, or a fresh salad.
8. Enjoy: Enjoy your homemade slavink with its delicious bacon-wrapped exterior and flavorful meatloaf filling!

Feel free to customize the meat mixture by adding herbs, spices, or other ingredients according to your taste preferences. Slavink is a versatile dish that can be enjoyed in various ways, so get creative and make it your own!

Gevulde Koek (Filled Almond Cookie)

Ingredients:

For the dough:

- 250g (about 2 cups) all-purpose flour
- 150g (about 2/3 cup) unsalted butter, softened
- 100g (about 1/2 cup) granulated sugar
- 1 large egg
- 1/2 teaspoon baking powder
- Pinch of salt
- 1/2 teaspoon almond extract

For the filling:

- 150g (about 1 cup) almond meal or ground almonds
- 100g (about 1/2 cup) granulated sugar
- 1 large egg
- 1 teaspoon almond extract

Additional:

- Sliced almonds or whole almonds for garnish (optional)
- Egg wash (1 egg beaten with a tablespoon of water)

Instructions:

1. Prepare the dough:
    - In a large mixing bowl, cream together the softened butter and sugar until light and fluffy.
    - Add the egg and almond extract to the butter mixture, and beat until well combined.
    - In a separate bowl, sift together the flour, baking powder, and salt. Gradually add the dry ingredients to the wet ingredients, mixing until a

smooth dough forms. Wrap the dough in plastic wrap and refrigerate for at least 30 minutes to firm up.
2. Make the filling:
    - In a mixing bowl, combine the almond meal (or ground almonds), sugar, egg, and almond extract. Mix until well combined. The filling should have a thick paste-like consistency. Set aside.
3. Preheat the oven: Preheat your oven to 180°C (350°F). Line a baking sheet with parchment paper.
4. Assemble the gevulde koek:
    - Divide the chilled dough into two equal portions. Roll out one portion of the dough on a lightly floured surface into a large circle, about 1/4 inch thick.
    - Transfer the rolled-out dough to the prepared baking sheet. Spread the almond paste filling evenly over the dough, leaving a small border around the edges.
    - Roll out the second portion of dough into a circle of similar size and place it on top of the almond paste filling.
    - Press the edges of the two dough circles together to seal in the filling. You can use a fork to crimp the edges for a decorative finish.
5. Decorate and bake:
    - Brush the top of the gevulde koek with the egg wash.
    - If desired, sprinkle sliced almonds or place whole almonds on top of the dough for garnish.
    - Using a sharp knife, make shallow diagonal cuts in the top of the dough to create a decorative pattern.
    - Bake in the preheated oven for 25-30 minutes, or until the gevulde koek is golden brown and cooked through.
6. Cool and serve:
    - Allow the gevulde koek to cool slightly on the baking sheet before transferring it to a wire rack to cool completely.
    - Once cooled, slice the gevulde koek into wedges or squares and serve with your favorite hot beverage.

Enjoy these homemade gevulde koek cookies with their delicious almond filling and buttery crust! They're perfect for sharing with family and friends or as a special treat for yourself.

Kroesjebrij (Fruit Pudding)

Ingredients:

- 100g (about 1/2 cup) pearl barley
- 1 liter (about 4 cups) water
- 100g (about 1/2 cup) dried fruits (raisins, currants, prunes, etc.)
- 50g (about 1/4 cup) sugar
- 1 cinnamon stick
- 3-4 whole cloves
- Pinch of salt
- Optional: lemon zest or orange zest for extra flavor

Instructions:

1. Prepare the barley: Rinse the pearl barley under cold water and drain. In a large saucepan, combine the rinsed barley with the water and bring to a boil over medium-high heat.
2. Cook the barley: Once the water is boiling, reduce the heat to low and simmer the barley, partially covered, for about 1 hour or until it is tender and has absorbed most of the water. Stir occasionally to prevent sticking.
3. Add the dried fruits: Once the barley is cooked, add the dried fruits, sugar, cinnamon stick, whole cloves, and a pinch of salt to the saucepan. Stir to combine.
4. Simmer the pudding: Continue to simmer the mixture over low heat, stirring occasionally, for an additional 30-45 minutes or until the fruits are plump and the pudding has thickened to your desired consistency. If the pudding becomes too thick, you can add a little more water to thin it out.
5. Remove from heat: Once the pudding has reached the desired consistency, remove the saucepan from the heat and discard the cinnamon stick and whole cloves. Taste and adjust the sweetness if needed by adding more sugar.
6. Serve: Ladle the warm Kroesjebrij into serving bowls or ramekins. You can serve it warm or chilled, depending on your preference. Garnish with a sprinkle of lemon or orange zest if desired.
7. Enjoy: Kroesjebrij is best enjoyed as a comforting dessert on its own or served with a dollop of whipped cream or a scoop of vanilla ice cream for added indulgence.

This homemade Kroesjebrij pudding is a delicious and comforting dessert that captures the flavors of traditional Dutch cuisine. Enjoy its rich and fruity taste as a delightful treat for any occasion!

Hangop (Dutch Curd)

Ingredients:

- 1 liter (about 4 cups) full-fat plain yogurt (preferably Greek yogurt or a yogurt with a high fat content)

Optional toppings:

- Fresh fruit (such as berries, sliced bananas, or peaches)
- Honey or maple syrup
- Cinnamon sugar
- Chopped nuts
- Granola

Instructions:

1. Prepare the yogurt: Place a large piece of cheesecloth or a clean kitchen towel over a large bowl or deep container. Spoon the plain yogurt onto the cheesecloth.
2. Strain the yogurt: Gather the edges of the cheesecloth and tie them together to form a bundle. Hang the bundle over the bowl or container so that the whey (liquid) can drip out. You can hang it from a kitchen faucet or use a wooden spoon to suspend it over the bowl.
3. Drain the whey: Allow the yogurt to strain for at least 4-6 hours, or preferably overnight, in the refrigerator. The longer you strain it, the thicker the hangop will become.
4. Transfer to a bowl: Once the yogurt has reached your desired consistency, remove the cheesecloth bundle and transfer the thickened hangop to a serving bowl.
5. Serve: Serve the hangop plain or with your choice of toppings. Fresh fruit, honey or maple syrup, cinnamon sugar, chopped nuts, and granola are popular options. You can also get creative with other toppings such as chocolate shavings, coconut flakes, or fruit preserves.
6. Enjoy: Enjoy your homemade hangop as a delicious and creamy dessert or snack!

Hangop is a versatile dish that can be customized to suit your taste preferences. Experiment with different flavors and toppings to create your own unique variations.

Whether enjoyed plain or dressed up with toppings, hangop is sure to be a hit with its rich and creamy texture and tangy flavor.

Advocaat (Dutch Eggnog)

Ingredients:

- 6 large egg yolks
- 200g (about 1 cup) granulated sugar
- 250ml (about 1 cup) brandy or cognac
- 1 teaspoon vanilla extract
- Pinch of salt
- Optional: grated nutmeg or ground cinnamon for garnish

Instructions:

1. Prepare a double boiler: Fill a saucepan with a few inches of water and bring it to a gentle simmer over medium heat. Place a heatproof bowl on top of the saucepan, ensuring that the bottom of the bowl does not touch the water.
2. Whisk egg yolks and sugar: In the heatproof bowl, whisk together the egg yolks and granulated sugar until smooth and well combined.
3. Cook the mixture: Gradually whisk in the brandy or cognac, vanilla extract, and a pinch of salt. Place the bowl over the simmering water and continue to whisk the mixture constantly for about 10-15 minutes, or until it thickens and coats the back of a spoon. Be careful not to let the mixture boil or the eggs will scramble.
4. Cool and strain: Once the mixture has thickened, remove the bowl from the heat and let it cool to room temperature. Strain the Advocaat through a fine-mesh sieve to remove any lumps or bits of cooked egg.
5. Bottle and chill: Transfer the strained Advocaat to a clean glass bottle or jar with a tight-fitting lid. Seal the bottle and refrigerate the Advocaat for at least 24 hours to allow the flavors to meld and the liqueur to thicken further.
6. Serve: Serve the Advocaat chilled in small glasses, garnished with a sprinkle of grated nutmeg or ground cinnamon if desired. Enjoy it as a luxurious dessert liqueur or use it as an ingredient in cocktails and desserts.

Homemade Advocaat is a delightful treat with its creamy texture and rich flavor. It's perfect for sipping on special occasions or sharing with friends and family during the holiday season. Cheers!

Spekdikken (Thick Pancakes with Bacon)

Ingredients:

- 250g (about 2 cups) all-purpose flour
- 2 teaspoons baking powder
- 1/2 teaspoon salt
- 2 large eggs
- 300ml (about 1 1/4 cups) milk
- 100g (about 1/2 cup) diced bacon or pancetta
- Butter or oil for frying

Optional toppings:

- Maple syrup
- Powdered sugar
- Applesauce

Instructions:

1. Prepare the batter:
    - In a large mixing bowl, whisk together the flour, baking powder, and salt until well combined.
    - In a separate bowl, beat the eggs and then add the milk. Whisk until smooth.
    - Gradually add the wet ingredients to the dry ingredients, stirring until a smooth batter forms. Let the batter rest for about 10-15 minutes.
2. Cook the bacon:
    - In a skillet or frying pan, cook the diced bacon over medium heat until it is crispy and golden brown. Remove the cooked bacon from the pan and drain on paper towels to remove excess grease.
3. Combine the batter and bacon:
    - Once the bacon is cooked and cooled slightly, fold it into the pancake batter until evenly distributed.
4. Cook the pancakes:
    - Heat a non-stick skillet or griddle over medium heat and add a small amount of butter or oil to grease the surface.

- Pour a ladleful of batter onto the skillet to form each pancake. Use the back of the ladle to spread the batter into a thick, round shape.
- Cook the pancakes for 2-3 minutes on each side, or until golden brown and cooked through. Flip the pancakes carefully using a spatula to ensure they cook evenly.

5. Serve:
    - Once cooked, transfer the Spekdikken to a serving plate and keep warm while you cook the remaining pancakes.
    - Serve the pancakes hot with your choice of toppings, such as maple syrup, powdered sugar, or applesauce.
6. Enjoy:
    - Enjoy your homemade Spekdikken as a delicious and hearty breakfast or brunch dish, perfect for cold winter mornings or special occasions!

Spekdikken are a delightful and comforting Dutch treat, with their savory bacon filling adding a unique and delicious twist to traditional pancakes. Serve them with your favorite toppings and enjoy their rich flavor and hearty texture!

Broodje Haring (Herring Sandwich)

Ingredients:

- 2 fresh herring fillets, cleaned and deboned
- 2 soft sandwich buns or rolls
- 1 small onion, finely chopped
- Pickles or pickled gherkins, thinly sliced
- Optional: Dutch mustard or mayonnaise
- Optional: Lemon wedges for serving

Instructions:

1. Prepare the herring fillets: Ensure the herring fillets are cleaned and deboned. If necessary, remove any scales and rinse the fillets under cold water. Pat them dry with paper towels.
2. Prepare the sandwich buns: Slice the sandwich buns or rolls in half horizontally, but not all the way through.
3. Assemble the sandwich:
    - Place a herring fillet on the bottom half of each bun.
    - Sprinkle the chopped onions over the herring fillets.
    - Add a few slices of pickles or pickled gherkins on top of the onions.
4. Optional toppings:
    - If desired, you can spread a thin layer of Dutch mustard or mayonnaise on the top half of the bun before placing it on top of the herring and toppings.
5. Serve:
    - Serve the Broodje Haring immediately, either open-faced or closed, depending on your preference.
    - Optionally, serve with lemon wedges on the side for squeezing over the herring.
6. Enjoy:
    - Enjoy your homemade Broodje Haring as a delicious and authentic Dutch snack, perfect for lunch or as a quick bite on the go!

Broodje Haring is a simple yet flavorful dish that highlights the freshness and natural flavor of herring, a staple ingredient in Dutch cuisine. With its combination of soft bread, tender herring, crunchy onions, and tangy pickles, it's sure to satisfy your cravings for a taste of the Netherlands!

Boterham met Kaas (Cheese Sandwich)

Ingredients:

- Sliced bread (whole wheat, white, or your preferred type)
- Sliced Dutch cheese (such as Gouda, Edam, or Maasdam)
- Butter (optional)
- Mustard (optional)
- Lettuce leaves (optional)
- Tomato slices (optional)

Instructions:

1. Prepare the bread:
    - Take two slices of your preferred bread. You can use whole wheat, white, or any other type of bread you prefer. Ensure the bread slices are fresh and not stale.
2. Slice the cheese:
    - Take a few slices of Dutch cheese, such as Gouda, Edam, or Maasdam. You can adjust the amount of cheese according to your preference and the size of your bread slices.
3. Assemble the sandwich:
    - If desired, spread a thin layer of butter on one or both slices of bread. This step is optional but can add extra flavor and richness to the sandwich.
    - Place the cheese slices on one slice of bread, ensuring they cover the entire surface evenly. You can add as many cheese slices as you like, depending on how cheesy you want your sandwich to be.
    - Optionally, spread a thin layer of mustard on the other slice of bread for added flavor. You can also add other optional ingredients such as lettuce leaves or tomato slices for extra freshness and texture.
4. Put it together:
    - Place the slice of bread with the cheese on top of the other slice, creating a sandwich. Press down gently to ensure the sandwich holds together.
5. Serve:
    - Your Boterham met kaas is now ready to be served! You can enjoy it as is or pair it with your favorite side dishes or accompaniments, such as a side salad, pickles, or chips.
6. Enjoy:

- Enjoy your homemade Boterham met kaas as a quick and satisfying snack or light meal, perfect for breakfast, lunch, or anytime you're craving something delicious and comforting!

Boterham met kaas is a versatile dish that can be customized to suit your taste preferences. Feel free to experiment with different types of cheese, bread, and additional toppings to create your own unique variations of this classic Dutch sandwich.

Droge Worst (Dried Sausage)

Ingredients:

- 1 kg (about 2.2 lbs) pork shoulder or beef chuck, finely ground
- 30g (about 2 tablespoons) kosher salt
- 10g (about 2 teaspoons) Prague powder #2 (curing salt)
- 10g (about 2 teaspoons) freshly ground black pepper
- 5g (about 1 teaspoon) ground coriander
- 5g (about 1 teaspoon) ground nutmeg
- 5g (about 1 teaspoon) garlic powder
- 5g (about 1 teaspoon) paprika
- 5g (about 1 teaspoon) sugar
- Natural sausage casings (hog casings or collagen casings)

Instructions:

1. Prepare the meat:
    - In a large mixing bowl, combine the finely ground pork or beef with all the spices and seasonings. Mix well until the spices are evenly distributed throughout the meat.
2. Stuff the casings:
    - Soak the natural sausage casings in cold water for about 30 minutes to soften them. Then, rinse them thoroughly under cold running water to remove any excess salt.
    - Using a sausage stuffer or a sausage-making attachment for a meat grinder, stuff the seasoned meat mixture into the casings, making sure to remove any air bubbles. Twist or tie off the casings at regular intervals to form individual sausages.
3. Fermentation:
    - Hang the stuffed sausages in a cool, dry place with good air circulation, such as a curing chamber or a well-ventilated cellar. Allow the sausages to ferment at room temperature (around 18-20°C or 65-68°F) for 24-48 hours. During this time, beneficial bacteria will develop, contributing to the flavor and texture of the sausages.
4. Drying:

- After the fermentation period, transfer the sausages to a dedicated drying chamber or a cool, well-ventilated area with low humidity. Hang the sausages vertically, ensuring they do not touch each other.
- Allow the sausages to dry for several weeks to several months, depending on your desired level of dryness and flavor intensity. The drying process can take anywhere from 4-12 weeks or even longer.

5. Storage:
   - Once the sausages have reached your desired level of dryness, they are ready to be enjoyed. Store the dried sausages in a cool, dry place or vacuum-seal them for longer-term storage in the refrigerator or freezer.
6. Slice and serve:
   - To serve droge worst, slice it thinly using a sharp knife. Enjoy the slices of dried sausage on their own as a snack, or pair them with bread, cheese, and your favorite condiments for a delicious appetizer or charcuterie board.

Homemade droge worst is a flavorful and satisfying snack that captures the essence of traditional Dutch cuisine. Experiment with different spice blends and drying times to create your own unique variations of this classic dried sausage.

Limburgse Vlaai (Limburg Flan)

Ingredients:

For the pastry crust:

- 300g (about 2 1/2 cups) all-purpose flour
- 150g (about 2/3 cup) unsalted butter, cold and diced
- 100g (about 1/2 cup) granulated sugar
- 1 large egg
- Pinch of salt

For the filling:

- 500ml (about 2 cups) milk
- 100g (about 1/2 cup) granulated sugar
- 40g (about 1/3 cup) cornstarch
- 3 large egg yolks
- 1 teaspoon vanilla extract
- Zest of 1 lemon (optional)

For the topping:

- Fresh fruit of your choice (cherries, apricots, plums, apples, etc.)
- Apricot jam or fruit glaze (optional, for brushing the fruit)

Instructions:

1. Prepare the pastry crust:
    - In a large mixing bowl, combine the flour, cold diced butter, sugar, egg, and a pinch of salt.
    - Use your fingers or a pastry cutter to rub the butter into the flour mixture until it resembles coarse crumbs and starts to come together.

- Turn the dough out onto a floured surface and knead briefly until it forms a smooth ball. Wrap the dough in plastic wrap and refrigerate for at least 30 minutes to firm up.
2. Preheat the oven: Preheat your oven to 180°C (350°F). Grease a 9-inch tart or pie pan.
3. Prepare the filling:
    - In a saucepan, heat the milk over medium heat until it just begins to simmer. Remove from heat.
    - In a separate mixing bowl, whisk together the sugar, cornstarch, and egg yolks until smooth.
    - Slowly pour the hot milk into the egg mixture, whisking constantly to prevent the eggs from scrambling.
    - Return the mixture to the saucepan and cook over medium heat, stirring constantly, until it thickens and coats the back of a spoon, about 5-7 minutes.
    - Remove from heat and stir in the vanilla extract and lemon zest, if using. Let the filling cool slightly.
4. Assemble the vlaai:
    - Roll out the chilled pastry dough on a floured surface to fit the size of your tart or pie pan. Transfer the dough to the prepared pan and press it gently into the bottom and sides.
    - Pour the slightly cooled filling into the pastry crust and spread it out evenly.
5. Add the fruit topping:
    - Arrange the fresh fruit on top of the filling in a decorative pattern. If desired, brush the fruit with apricot jam or fruit glaze to give it a glossy finish.
6. Bake the vlaai:
    - Place the vlaai in the preheated oven and bake for 30-35 minutes, or until the crust is golden brown and the filling is set.
    - Remove from the oven and let the vlaai cool completely in the pan before slicing and serving.
7. Serve and enjoy:
    - Once cooled, slice the Limburgse vlaai into wedges and serve it as a delicious dessert or sweet treat for any occasion.

Limburgse vlaai is best enjoyed fresh on the day it's made, but any leftovers can be stored in an airtight container in the refrigerator for up to a few days. Enjoy the sweet and creamy goodness of this traditional Dutch pastry!

Pannenkoeken (Dutch Pancakes)

Ingredients:

- 250g (about 2 cups) all-purpose flour
- 500ml (about 2 cups) milk
- 2 large eggs
- Pinch of salt
- Butter or oil for frying

Optional toppings:

- Powdered sugar
- Maple syrup
- Honey
- Fresh fruit (such as sliced strawberries, bananas, or blueberries)
- Jam or preserves
- Nutella or chocolate spread
- Cheese (such as Gouda or Edam)
- Bacon or ham
- Savory vegetables (such as spinach, mushrooms, or bell peppers)

Instructions:

1. Prepare the batter:
    - In a large mixing bowl, whisk together the flour and salt.
    - In a separate bowl, beat the eggs, then gradually whisk in the milk until smooth.
    - Slowly pour the wet ingredients into the flour mixture, whisking continuously until you have a smooth batter without any lumps. The consistency should be similar to heavy cream. If the batter is too thick, you can add a little more milk to thin it out.
2. Let the batter rest:
    - Cover the bowl with plastic wrap or a clean kitchen towel and let the batter rest at room temperature for about 30 minutes. This allows the flour to fully hydrate and helps ensure tender pancakes.
3. Cook the pancakes:

- Heat a non-stick skillet or frying pan over medium heat. Add a small amount of butter or oil to the pan and swirl it around to coat the bottom evenly.
- Once the pan is hot, pour a ladleful of batter into the center of the pan, tilting and swirling the pan to spread the batter into a thin, even layer.
- Cook the pancake for 1-2 minutes, or until the edges start to lift and the bottom is golden brown. Use a spatula to flip the pancake and cook for another 1-2 minutes on the other side, until golden brown and cooked through.
- Transfer the cooked pancake to a plate and cover with a clean kitchen towel to keep warm. Repeat with the remaining batter, adding more butter or oil to the pan as needed.

4. Serve with toppings:
    - Once all the pancakes are cooked, serve them warm with your choice of toppings. Traditional sweet toppings include powdered sugar, maple syrup, honey, or fresh fruit. For a savory twist, you can fill the pancakes with cheese, bacon, or vegetables.
5. Enjoy:
    - Enjoy your homemade Dutch pannenkoeken as a delicious and versatile meal or snack, perfect for any time of day!

Dutch pancakes are highly customizable, so feel free to experiment with different toppings and fillings to create your own unique variations. Whether sweet or savory, pannenkoeken are sure to be a hit with their thin, fluffy texture and delicious flavor!

Krentenwegge (Currant Loaf)

Ingredients:

- 500g (about 4 cups) all-purpose flour
- 7g (about 2 1/4 teaspoons) instant yeast
- 100g (about 1/2 cup) granulated sugar
- 1 teaspoon salt
- 1 teaspoon ground cinnamon
- 1/2 teaspoon ground cloves
- 250ml (about 1 cup) warm milk
- 75g (about 1/3 cup) unsalted butter, melted
- 1 large egg
- 200g (about 1 1/3 cups) currants or raisins
- Egg wash (1 egg beaten with a tablespoon of water)

Instructions:

1. Activate the yeast:
   - In a small bowl, mix together the warm milk and instant yeast. Let it sit for about 5-10 minutes until foamy.
2. Prepare the dough:
   - In a large mixing bowl, combine the flour, sugar, salt, cinnamon, and ground cloves.
   - Make a well in the center of the dry ingredients and pour in the yeast mixture, melted butter, and beaten egg.
   - Stir the ingredients together until a soft dough forms.
3. Knead the dough:
   - Turn the dough out onto a lightly floured surface and knead it for about 8-10 minutes, or until it becomes smooth and elastic. You can also use a stand mixer fitted with a dough hook for this step.
4. Add the currants:
   - Flatten the dough slightly and sprinkle the currants or raisins evenly over the surface.
   - Fold the dough over the currants and continue kneading until they are evenly distributed throughout the dough.
5. First rise:

- Place the dough in a greased bowl, cover it with a clean kitchen towel or plastic wrap, and let it rise in a warm, draft-free place for about 1-1.5 hours, or until it doubles in size.
6. Shape the loaf:
    - Once the dough has risen, punch it down to release the air and transfer it to a lightly floured surface.
    - Shape the dough into a loaf by rolling it out into a rectangle and then rolling it up tightly, starting from one of the long sides.
7. Second rise:
    - Place the shaped loaf on a parchment-lined baking sheet and cover it loosely with a clean kitchen towel. Let it rise for another 45-60 minutes, or until it doubles in size.
8. Preheat the oven:
    - Meanwhile, preheat your oven to 180°C (350°F).
9. Brush with egg wash:
    - Once the loaf has finished its second rise, brush the surface with the egg wash to give it a shiny finish.
10. Bake the loaf:
    - Bake the Krentenwegge in the preheated oven for 30-35 minutes, or until it is golden brown and sounds hollow when tapped on the bottom.
11. Cool and serve:
    - Allow the loaf to cool on a wire rack before slicing and serving. Enjoy your homemade Krentenwegge with butter or on its own as a delicious sweet treat!

Krentenwegge is best enjoyed fresh on the day it's made, but any leftovers can be stored in an airtight container at room temperature for a few days or frozen for longer-term storage. Enjoy the sweet and spicy flavors of this traditional Dutch currant loaf with your family and friends!

Slavinken (Bacon-wrapped Ground Meat Rolls)

Ingredients:

- 500g (about 1 lb) ground meat (a mixture of beef and pork)
- 8-10 slices of bacon
- Salt and pepper to taste
- Ground nutmeg or other spices (optional)
- Butter or oil for frying

Instructions:

1. Prepare the meat mixture:
    - In a mixing bowl, combine the ground meat with salt, pepper, and any additional spices you like, such as ground nutmeg. Mix well until the seasonings are evenly distributed throughout the meat.
2. Shape the Slavinken:
    - Divide the seasoned meat mixture into 8-10 equal portions, depending on the size of Slavinken you prefer.
    - Take each portion of meat and shape it into a small sausage-like roll, about 2-3 inches long.
3. Wrap with bacon:
    - Take a slice of bacon and wrap it tightly around each meat roll, securing the ends with toothpicks if necessary to hold the bacon in place.
4. Cook the Slavinken:
    - Heat a skillet or frying pan over medium heat and add a little butter or oil.
    - Once the skillet is hot, add the Slavinken and cook them for 3-4 minutes on each side, or until the bacon is crispy and the meat is cooked through. Turn them occasionally to ensure even cooking.
5. Serve:
    - Once the Slavinken are cooked, remove them from the skillet and drain on paper towels to remove any excess grease.
    - Serve the Slavinken hot, with your choice of side dishes such as mashed potatoes, steamed vegetables, or a fresh salad.
6. Enjoy:
    - Enjoy your homemade Slavinken as a delicious and satisfying meal, perfect for a cozy dinner with family or friends!

Slavinken are versatile and can be customized to suit your taste preferences. You can experiment with different seasonings and variations, such as adding minced onions or garlic to the meat mixture, or using different types of bacon for wrapping. However you make them, Slavinken are sure to be a hit with their savory flavor and satisfying texture.

Kapsalon (Meat, French Fries, and Salad)

Ingredients:

- 500g (about 1 lb) French fries
- 300g (about 10 oz) seasoned meat (such as shawarma, kebab, or gyro meat)
- 150g (about 1 1/2 cups) grated cheese (such as Gouda or Cheddar)
- 1 small onion, thinly sliced
- 1 tomato, diced
- 1/2 cucumber, thinly sliced
- Handful of shredded lettuce or mixed salad greens
- Garlic sauce and/or sambal sauce, to taste
- Olive oil
- Salt and pepper, to taste

Instructions:

1. Prepare the French fries:
    - If using frozen French fries, follow the instructions on the package to cook them until they are golden and crispy. You can also make homemade French fries by cutting potatoes into thin strips, frying them until golden brown, and draining them on paper towels.
2. Cook the seasoned meat:
    - Heat a skillet over medium heat and add a splash of olive oil. Cook the seasoned meat until it is browned and cooked through, breaking it apart with a spatula as it cooks. Season with salt and pepper to taste.
3. Assemble the Kapsalon:
    - Preheat your oven to 200°C (400°F).
    - Spread the cooked French fries in an even layer in a baking dish or oven-safe skillet.
    - Top the fries with the cooked seasoned meat, spreading it out evenly.
    - Sprinkle the grated cheese over the meat layer, covering it completely.
4. Bake the Kapsalon:
    - Place the baking dish or skillet in the preheated oven and bake for 5-7 minutes, or until the cheese is melted and bubbly.
5. Add the salad ingredients:

- Remove the Kapsalon from the oven and top it with the thinly sliced onion, diced tomato, sliced cucumber, and shredded lettuce or mixed salad greens.
6. Drizzle with sauce:
    - Drizzle the Kapsalon with garlic sauce and/or sambal sauce, according to your taste preferences.
7. Serve:
    - Serve the Kapsalon hot, straight from the oven, as a satisfying and flavorful meal. Enjoy the crispy French fries, savory seasoned meat, melted cheese, and fresh salad ingredients all in one delicious dish!

Kapsalon is a versatile dish, so feel free to customize it with your favorite ingredients and toppings. Whether enjoyed as a quick weeknight dinner or as a crowd-pleasing dish for a casual gathering, Kapsalon is sure to be a hit with its bold flavors and comforting appeal.

Zeeuwse Bolus (Sweet Pastry)

Ingredients:

- 500g (about 4 cups) all-purpose flour
- 1 packet (7g) active dry yeast
- 250ml (about 1 cup) lukewarm milk
- 75g (about 1/3 cup) unsalted butter, melted
- 75g (about 1/3 cup) granulated sugar
- 1 teaspoon salt
- 1 teaspoon ground cinnamon
- 100g (about 1/2 cup) dark brown sugar
- 100g (about 1/2 cup) granulated sugar
- 1 tablespoon ground cinnamon
- 100g (about 1/2 cup) unsalted butter, softened
- Water, as needed

Instructions:

1. Activate the yeast:
    - In a small bowl, dissolve the yeast in the lukewarm milk. Let it sit for about 5-10 minutes until it becomes frothy.
2. Prepare the dough:
    - In a large mixing bowl, combine the flour, melted butter, granulated sugar, salt, and ground cinnamon.
    - Pour in the activated yeast mixture and mix until a dough forms.
    - Knead the dough on a floured surface for about 5-7 minutes, or until it becomes smooth and elastic. Add more flour if the dough is too sticky.
3. First rise:
    - Place the dough in a greased bowl, cover it with a clean kitchen towel or plastic wrap, and let it rise in a warm, draft-free place for about 1 hour, or until it doubles in size.
4. Prepare the filling:
    - In a small bowl, mix together the dark brown sugar, granulated sugar, and ground cinnamon.
5. Shape the bolus:
    - Punch down the risen dough and divide it into 12 equal portions.

- Roll each portion of dough into a rope, about 30-35cm (12-14 inches) long.
- Spread a thin layer of softened butter over each rope of dough, then sprinkle the cinnamon sugar mixture evenly over the butter.

6. Form the spiral shape:
    - Starting from one end, roll up each rope of dough tightly into a spiral shape, similar to a cinnamon roll.
    - Place the shaped boluses on a baking sheet lined with parchment paper, leaving some space between them to allow for rising.
7. Second rise:
    - Cover the shaped boluses with a clean kitchen towel and let them rise in a warm, draft-free place for another 30-45 minutes, or until they double in size.
8. Bake the boluses:
    - Preheat your oven to 200°C (400°F).
    - Once the boluses have risen, lightly brush them with water to help create a sticky surface.
    - Bake in the preheated oven for 15-20 minutes, or until they are golden brown and cooked through.
9. Serve and enjoy:
    - Allow the Zeeuwse boluses to cool slightly before serving. Enjoy them warm with a cup of coffee or tea for a delightful treat!

Zeeuwse bolus is best enjoyed fresh on the day it's made, but any leftovers can be stored in an airtight container at room temperature for a day or two. Enjoy the sticky sweetness and comforting flavors of this traditional Dutch pastry!

Balkenbrij (Sausage made from Pork)

Ingredients:

- 500g (about 1 lb) pork liver
- 250g (about 1/2 lb) pork heart and/or kidneys (optional)
- 1 onion, finely chopped
- 100g (about 1/2 cup) buckwheat flour
- 50g (about 1/4 cup) barley or oats
- 1 teaspoon ground cloves
- 1 teaspoon ground nutmeg
- Salt and pepper, to taste
- Water or broth, as needed
- Butter or oil, for frying

Instructions:

1. Prepare the offal:
    - Rinse the pork liver, heart, and kidneys (if using) under cold water and pat them dry with paper towels. Trim off any excess fat or connective tissue.
    - Cut the offal into smaller pieces and place them in a large pot or saucepan.
2. Cook the offal:
    - Add enough water or broth to the pot to cover the offal completely.
    - Bring the liquid to a boil over high heat, then reduce the heat to low and simmer the offal for about 1-1.5 hours, or until it is tender and fully cooked.
    - Remove the offal from the pot and let it cool slightly. Reserve the cooking liquid for later use.
3. Prepare the mixture:
    - In a food processor or blender, pulse the cooked offal until it is finely chopped but not completely smooth.
    - Transfer the chopped offal to a mixing bowl and add the finely chopped onion, buckwheat flour, barley or oats, ground cloves, ground nutmeg, salt, and pepper. Mix until well combined.
4. Cook the mixture:
    - Return the offal mixture to the pot along with a portion of the reserved cooking liquid (about 1-2 cups). The mixture should have a thick, porridge-like consistency.

- Cook the mixture over low heat, stirring constantly, for about 30-45 minutes, or until it thickens and the flavors meld together. Add more cooking liquid as needed to prevent it from drying out.
5. Pour into molds:
    - Once the mixture has thickened, pour it into greased molds or loaf pans. Smooth the top with a spatula and let it cool to room temperature.
6. Slice and fry:
    - Once cooled and solidified, slice the balkenbrij into thick slices.
    - Heat a skillet or frying pan over medium heat and add a knob of butter or a drizzle of oil.
    - Fry the balkenbrij slices for 3-4 minutes on each side, or until they are golden brown and crispy on the outside.
7. Serve and enjoy:
    - Serve the fried balkenbrij slices hot as a delicious and hearty dish, accompanied by mustard or pickles if desired.

Balkenbrij is a unique and flavorful dish that's perfect for enjoying on cold winter days or as part of a traditional Dutch meal. Experiment with the spices and seasonings to customize the flavor to your liking!

Arretjescake (Chocolate Biscuit Cake)

Ingredients:

- 200g (about 7 oz) dark chocolate (at least 70% cocoa), chopped
- 200g (about 7 oz) unsalted butter
- 200g (about 1 cup) granulated sugar
- 200g (about 7 oz) plain biscuits or cookies (such as Marie biscuits or digestive biscuits), crushed into small pieces
- Cocoa powder, for dusting (optional)
- Parchment paper, for lining the loaf pan

Instructions:

1. Melt the chocolate and butter:
    - In a heatproof bowl set over a pot of simmering water (double boiler method), melt the chopped dark chocolate and unsalted butter together, stirring occasionally until smooth and well combined. Alternatively, you can melt them together in the microwave in short bursts, stirring in between each burst until melted and smooth.
2. Mix in the sugar:
    - Once the chocolate and butter are melted and combined, remove the bowl from the heat source.
    - Stir in the granulated sugar until it's completely dissolved and incorporated into the chocolate mixture.
3. Combine with crushed biscuits:
    - Add the crushed biscuits or cookies to the chocolate mixture, stirring until they are evenly coated and well combined. The mixture should be thick and sticky.
4. Shape and chill the cake:
    - Line a loaf pan with parchment paper, leaving some overhang on the sides for easy removal.
    - Transfer the chocolate biscuit mixture into the prepared loaf pan, pressing it down firmly and smoothing the top with a spatula.
    - Place the loaf pan in the refrigerator and chill the Arretjescake for at least 4 hours, or until it's firm and set.
5. Slice and serve:

- Once chilled and set, remove the Arretjescake from the loaf pan using the parchment paper overhang.
- Place it on a cutting board and slice it into thick bars or squares using a sharp knife.
- Optionally, dust the top of the cake with cocoa powder before serving for a decorative touch.

6. Enjoy:
    - Serve the Arretjescake chilled or at room temperature as a delightful and indulgent dessert or sweet snack. Store any leftovers in an airtight container in the refrigerator for up to a week.

Arretjescake is incredibly versatile, and you can customize it by adding nuts, dried fruits, or spices to the chocolate biscuit mixture according to your taste preferences. Whether enjoyed on its own or paired with your favorite hot beverage, Arretjescake is sure to be a hit with its rich chocolate flavor and satisfying crunch!

Hagel & Wit (Bread with Hagelslag and Butter)

Ingredients:

- Slices of white bread or soft rolls
- Butter, at room temperature
- Hagelslag (chocolate sprinkles)

Instructions:

1. Prepare the bread:
   - Start by selecting your choice of white bread slices or soft rolls. You can toast the bread if you prefer a warm and crispy texture, or leave it untoasted for a softer bite.
2. Spread with butter:
   - Spread a generous amount of butter on each slice of bread or each half of the soft roll. The butter should cover the surface evenly to provide a creamy base for the hagelslag.
3. Add the hagelslag:
   - Sprinkle a thick layer of hagelslag (chocolate sprinkles) over the buttered bread or roll. Make sure to cover the entire surface with the chocolate sprinkles for maximum flavor.
4. Serve and enjoy:
   - Once the hagelslag is evenly distributed over the buttered bread, your Hagel & Wit is ready to be enjoyed! Serve it as a quick breakfast, snack, or even as a sweet treat for dessert.

Hagel & Wit is a delightful combination of creamy butter, rich chocolate, and soft bread, providing a perfect balance of flavors and textures. It's a beloved Dutch snack that's simple to make and sure to satisfy your sweet cravings any time of day!

Haringsalade (Herring Salad)

Ingredients:

- 400g (about 14 oz) pickled herring fillets, diced
- 500g (about 1 lb) potatoes, boiled and diced
- 1 small onion, finely chopped
- 2-3 pickles, diced
- 2 tablespoons fresh dill, chopped (optional, for garnish)
- Salt and pepper, to taste

For the dressing:

- 150ml (about 2/3 cup) mayonnaise
- 2 tablespoons sour cream or Greek yogurt
- 1 tablespoon Dijon mustard
- 1 tablespoon white wine vinegar
- 1 teaspoon sugar
- Salt and pepper, to taste

Instructions:

1. Prepare the dressing:
   - In a small bowl, whisk together the mayonnaise, sour cream or Greek yogurt, Dijon mustard, white wine vinegar, sugar, salt, and pepper until smooth and well combined. Adjust the seasoning to taste.
2. Assemble the salad:
   - In a large mixing bowl, combine the diced pickled herring, boiled and diced potatoes, chopped onion, and diced pickles.
3. Add the dressing:
   - Pour the dressing over the herring and potato mixture, and gently toss until everything is evenly coated with the dressing.
4. Chill the salad:
   - Cover the bowl with plastic wrap or transfer the salad to an airtight container, and refrigerate for at least 1 hour to allow the flavors to meld together and the salad to chill.
5. Serve:

- Once chilled, remove the haringsalade from the refrigerator and give it a final toss.
- Transfer the salad to a serving dish and garnish with chopped fresh dill, if desired.
6. Enjoy:
    - Serve the haringsalade as a refreshing and flavorful appetizer or side dish, alongside crusty bread or crackers. It's best enjoyed cold, straight from the refrigerator.

Haringsalade is a classic Dutch dish that showcases the beloved pickled herring in a delicious and satisfying salad. Feel free to customize the salad by adding other ingredients such as boiled eggs, apples, or capers according to your taste preferences.

Ossenworst (Raw Beef Sausage)

Ingredients:

- 500g (about 1 lb) high-quality beef, such as sirloin or tenderloin, trimmed of fat and sinew
- 1 teaspoon salt
- 1/2 teaspoon ground white pepper
- 1/4 teaspoon ground cloves
- 1/4 teaspoon ground nutmeg
- 1 clove garlic, minced (optional)
- Natural beef casings (if available)

Instructions:

1. Prepare the beef:
   - Cut the beef into small cubes and place them in the freezer for about 30 minutes to firm up slightly. This will make it easier to grind.
2. Grind the beef:
   - Using a meat grinder or food processor fitted with a grinding attachment, grind the chilled beef cubes into a fine texture. Alternatively, you can ask your butcher to grind the beef for you.
3. Season the beef:
   - In a large mixing bowl, combine the ground beef with salt, white pepper, ground cloves, ground nutmeg, and minced garlic (if using). Mix well until the seasonings are evenly distributed throughout the meat.
4. Shape the ossenworst:
   - If using natural beef casings, rinse them thoroughly under cold water and soak them in warm water for about 30 minutes to soften.
   - Stuff the seasoned beef mixture into the beef casings, if using, using a sausage stuffer or a piping bag fitted with a large round tip. Alternatively, you can shape the mixture into logs or patties without casings.
5. Cure the ossenworst (optional):
   - If desired, you can cure the ossenworst by wrapping it tightly in plastic wrap or parchment paper and refrigerating it for 1-2 days. This step helps to develop the flavor and texture of the sausage.
6. Serve and enjoy:

- Once cured (if applicable), slice the ossenworst thinly and serve it as a cold appetizer or snack. It pairs well with crusty bread, mustard, pickles, and other traditional Dutch accompaniments.

Ossenworst is best enjoyed fresh and should be stored in the refrigerator. It can also be frozen for longer-term storage, but the texture may change slightly upon thawing. Adjust the seasoning according to your taste preferences, and experiment with different spices to create your own unique version of this traditional Dutch delicacy.

Kippensoep (Chicken Soup)

Ingredients:

- 1 whole chicken (about 1.5-2 kg or 3-4 lbs), skin removed and cut into pieces
- 2 onions, peeled and quartered
- 3 carrots, peeled and chopped into chunks
- 3 celery stalks, chopped into chunks
- 2-3 cloves of garlic, peeled and smashed
- 1 bay leaf
- 1 teaspoon whole peppercorns
- Salt, to taste
- Fresh parsley, chopped, for garnish (optional)

Instructions:

1. Prepare the chicken:
    - Rinse the chicken pieces under cold water and pat them dry with paper towels. Remove the skin and excess fat from the chicken pieces.
2. Simmer the chicken:
    - In a large stockpot, add the chicken pieces, quartered onions, chopped carrots, chopped celery, smashed garlic cloves, bay leaf, and whole peppercorns.
    - Pour enough water into the pot to cover the chicken and vegetables by a couple of inches. Season with salt to taste.
3. Bring to a boil:
    - Place the stockpot over medium-high heat and bring the mixture to a boil. Once boiling, reduce the heat to low and let the soup simmer gently, uncovered, for about 1-1.5 hours, or until the chicken is cooked through and the flavors have developed.
4. Skim off any foam:
    - As the soup simmers, you may notice foam rising to the surface. Use a ladle or spoon to skim off any foam and impurities that accumulate on top of the soup.
5. Remove the chicken:
    - Once the chicken is cooked through and tender, use tongs to remove the chicken pieces from the soup and transfer them to a plate or cutting board. Let them cool slightly before handling.

6. Shred the chicken:
    - Once cooled, shred the chicken meat using your fingers or a fork, discarding any bones or cartilage. You can shred the chicken into bite-sized pieces or larger chunks, depending on your preference.
7. Return chicken to the soup:
    - Return the shredded chicken meat to the soup and stir to combine. Taste and adjust the seasoning with salt, if needed.
8. Serve:
    - Ladle the kippensoep into bowls and garnish with chopped fresh parsley, if desired. Serve hot and enjoy!

Kippensoep is delicious on its own or served with crusty bread or crackers for a more substantial meal. It's a versatile dish, so feel free to customize it by adding other vegetables, herbs, or spices according to your taste preferences.

Vlaflip (Dessert with Custard and Yogurt)

Ingredients:

- 500ml (about 2 cups) custard (store-bought or homemade)
- 500ml (about 2 cups) yogurt (plain or flavored, such as vanilla or fruit)
- Fruit compote or syrup (such as raspberry, strawberry, or cherry)
- Fresh fruit, for garnish (optional)
- Whipped cream, for garnish (optional)
- Sprinkles or chocolate shavings, for garnish (optional)

Instructions:

1. Prepare the custard:
    - If using store-bought custard, simply transfer it to a bowl and set it aside. If making homemade custard, follow your favorite custard recipe and let it cool completely before using.
2. Prepare the yogurt:
    - If using plain yogurt, you can sweeten it to taste with a little honey or sugar, if desired. If using flavored yogurt, such as vanilla or fruit-flavored yogurt, simply transfer it to a bowl and set it aside.
3. Assemble the vlaflip:
    - Start by spooning a layer of custard into the bottom of each serving glass or bowl, filling it about one-third of the way full.
    - Next, add a layer of yogurt on top of the custard, filling the glass or bowl about two-thirds of the way full.
    - Finally, add a layer of fruit compote or syrup on top of the yogurt, filling the glass or bowl almost to the top.
4. Garnish the vlaflip:
    - If desired, garnish the vlaflip with fresh fruit, whipped cream, sprinkles, or chocolate shavings for an extra special touch.
5. Serve and enjoy:
    - Serve the vlaflip immediately, or refrigerate it for a few hours to allow the flavors to meld together and the dessert to chill.
    - Use long spoons to reach all the layers as you enjoy this delicious and refreshing Dutch dessert.

Vlaflip is a versatile dessert, so feel free to customize it with your favorite flavors of custard, yogurt, and fruit compote or syrup. You can also experiment with different combinations of fruits and toppings to create your own unique vlaflip creation. Whether enjoyed as a dessert or a sweet snack, vlaflip is sure to be a hit with its creamy texture and delightful layers of flavor!

Boerenjongens (Brandy-infused Raisins)

Ingredients:

- 250g (about 1 1/2 cups) raisins
- 250ml (about 1 cup) brandy or another strong liquor (such as rum or whiskey)
- 100g (about 1/2 cup) granulated sugar
- 1 cinnamon stick
- 3-4 whole cloves
- Zest of 1 lemon (optional)

Instructions:

1. Prepare the raisins:
   - Place the raisins in a clean glass jar or container with a tight-fitting lid.
2. Make the spiced syrup:
   - In a small saucepan, combine the brandy, granulated sugar, cinnamon stick, whole cloves, and lemon zest (if using).
   - Heat the mixture over medium heat, stirring occasionally, until the sugar has completely dissolved and the mixture comes to a gentle simmer. Remove from heat.
3. Infuse the raisins:
   - Carefully pour the hot spiced syrup over the raisins in the jar, making sure they are completely submerged.
   - Seal the jar tightly with the lid and let it cool to room temperature.
4. Store and age:
   - Once cooled, store the jar of boerenjongens in a cool, dark place, such as a pantry or cupboard.
   - Allow the raisins to soak in the brandy mixture for at least a few days, but preferably for several weeks or even months. The longer the raisins soak, the more flavorful they will become.
5. Serve and enjoy:
   - Once the boerenjongens have aged to your liking, they are ready to be enjoyed.
   - Serve them as a sweet and boozy topping for desserts such as ice cream, yogurt, pancakes, or cakes.
   - You can also enjoy boerenjongens on their own as a delightful and indulgent treat.

Boerenjongens can be stored in the refrigerator for an extended period, and the flavors will continue to develop over time. Just be sure to keep the jar tightly sealed when not in use to prevent evaporation of the alcohol. Enjoy this traditional Dutch delicacy as a special treat or gift it to friends and family for a unique culinary experience!

Romige Aspergesoep (Creamy Asparagus Soup)

Ingredients:

- 500g (about 1 lb) fresh asparagus
- 1 onion, chopped
- 2 cloves garlic, minced
- 2 tablespoons unsalted butter
- 2 tablespoons all-purpose flour
- 1 liter (about 4 cups) vegetable or chicken broth
- 250ml (about 1 cup) heavy cream
- Salt and pepper, to taste
- Fresh chives or parsley, chopped, for garnish (optional)

Instructions:

1. Prepare the asparagus:
    - Wash the asparagus spears under cold water and trim off the tough ends. Cut the asparagus into 1-inch pieces, reserving the tips for garnish if desired.
2. Sauté the aromatics:
    - In a large pot or Dutch oven, melt the butter over medium heat. Add the chopped onion and minced garlic, and sauté until softened and fragrant, about 3-5 minutes.
3. Cook the asparagus:
    - Add the chopped asparagus (excluding the tips) to the pot with the onions and garlic. Cook for another 5 minutes, stirring occasionally, until the asparagus begins to soften.
4. Make the roux:
    - Sprinkle the flour over the cooked asparagus and stir to combine, creating a roux. Cook for an additional 2-3 minutes to cook off the raw flour taste.
5. Simmer the soup:
    - Gradually pour in the vegetable or chicken broth, stirring constantly to prevent lumps from forming. Bring the mixture to a simmer and cook for about 15-20 minutes, or until the asparagus is tender.
6. Blend the soup:
    - Using an immersion blender or working in batches with a regular blender, puree the soup until smooth and creamy.

7. Add the cream:
    - Stir in the heavy cream, and season the soup with salt and pepper to taste. If using, add the asparagus tips and cook for an additional 2-3 minutes, until the tips are tender but still bright green.
8. Serve:
    - Ladle the creamy asparagus soup into bowls and garnish with chopped fresh chives or parsley, if desired. Serve hot and enjoy!

Romige aspergesoep is best enjoyed fresh, but any leftovers can be stored in an airtight container in the refrigerator for up to 3-4 days. Reheat gently on the stove before serving. Serve this creamy and flavorful soup as a starter or light meal, accompanied by crusty bread or a side salad for a complete and satisfying dish.

Oosterse Groentensoep (Oriental Vegetable Soup)

Ingredients:

- 1 liter (about 4 cups) vegetable or chicken broth
- 2 cups water
- 2 carrots, peeled and thinly sliced
- 1 bell pepper, thinly sliced
- 1 cup sliced mushrooms
- 1 cup shredded cabbage or bok choy
- 1 cup snow peas, trimmed
- 1 small onion, finely chopped
- 2 cloves garlic, minced
- 1-inch piece of ginger, peeled and grated
- 2 tablespoons soy sauce
- 1 tablespoon rice vinegar
- 1 tablespoon sesame oil
- 1 teaspoon chili paste or sriracha (optional, adjust to taste)
- Salt and pepper, to taste
- Fresh cilantro or green onions, chopped, for garnish (optional)

Instructions:

1. Prepare the vegetables:
   - Wash and prepare all the vegetables as directed. Slice the carrots, bell pepper, mushrooms, and snow peas thinly. Finely chop the onion, mince the garlic, and grate the ginger.
2. Sauté the aromatics:
   - In a large pot or Dutch oven, heat a bit of oil over medium heat. Add the chopped onion, minced garlic, and grated ginger. Sauté for 2-3 minutes until fragrant.
3. Add the vegetables:
   - Add the sliced carrots, bell pepper, mushrooms, and shredded cabbage or bok choy to the pot. Cook for another 3-4 minutes, stirring occasionally, until the vegetables begin to soften.
4. Add the broth and seasonings:

- Pour in the vegetable or chicken broth and water. Stir in the soy sauce, rice vinegar, sesame oil, and chili paste or sriracha (if using). Season with salt and pepper to taste.
5. Simmer the soup:
    - Bring the soup to a boil, then reduce the heat to low and let it simmer for about 10-15 minutes, or until the vegetables are tender but still slightly crisp.
6. Adjust the seasoning:
    - Taste the soup and adjust the seasoning as needed. Add more soy sauce, rice vinegar, or chili paste to adjust the flavor to your liking.
7. Serve:
    - Ladle the Oosterse groentensoep into bowls and garnish with chopped fresh cilantro or green onions, if desired. Serve hot and enjoy!

This Oosterse groentensoep is a versatile dish, and you can customize it by adding other vegetables such as bean sprouts, baby corn, or broccoli florets. You can also add cooked chicken, tofu, or shrimp for extra protein. Enjoy this flavorful and nutritious soup as a light meal or starter for your next Asian-inspired dinner!

Babi Pangang (Indonesian-style Pork Dish)

Ingredients:

For the pork:

- 500g (about 1 lb) pork tenderloin or pork shoulder, thinly sliced or cut into bite-sized pieces
- 2 cloves garlic, minced
- 1 tablespoon ginger, grated
- 2 tablespoons soy sauce
- 1 tablespoon hoisin sauce
- 1 tablespoon honey or brown sugar
- Salt and pepper, to taste
- Vegetable oil, for frying

For the sauce:

- 1/4 cup tomato ketchup
- 2 tablespoons soy sauce
- 2 tablespoons hoisin sauce
- 2 tablespoons honey or brown sugar
- 1 tablespoon rice vinegar or white vinegar
- 1 teaspoon sesame oil
- 1 teaspoon grated ginger
- 2 cloves garlic, minced
- 1 tablespoon cornstarch, dissolved in 2 tablespoons water

For serving:

- Steamed rice
- Sliced green onions, for garnish
- Sesame seeds, for garnish (optional)

Instructions:

1. Marinate the pork:
   - In a bowl, combine the minced garlic, grated ginger, soy sauce, hoisin sauce, honey or brown sugar, salt, and pepper. Add the sliced pork to the marinade, ensuring it is well coated. Cover and refrigerate for at least 30 minutes, or overnight for best results.
2. Prepare the sauce:
   - In a small saucepan, combine the tomato ketchup, soy sauce, hoisin sauce, honey or brown sugar, rice vinegar, sesame oil, grated ginger, and minced garlic. Bring the mixture to a simmer over medium heat.
   - Stir in the cornstarch slurry and cook for 1-2 minutes, or until the sauce has thickened. Remove from heat and set aside.
3. Cook the pork:
   - Heat some vegetable oil in a large skillet or wok over medium-high heat. Once hot, add the marinated pork in batches, ensuring not to overcrowd the pan. Cook until the pork is golden brown and crispy on all sides, about 3-4 minutes per side. Remove the cooked pork from the pan and drain on paper towels.
4. Assemble the dish:
   - Arrange the cooked pork on a serving platter. Drizzle the prepared sauce over the pork or serve it on the side for dipping.
5. Serve:
   - Garnish with sliced green onions and sesame seeds, if desired. Serve the Babi Pangang hot with steamed rice on the side.

Babi Pangang is a delicious and satisfying dish that pairs well with steamed rice and vegetables. Adjust the seasonings and sweetness of the sauce according to your taste preferences. Enjoy this Indonesian-inspired pork dish as a flavorful main course for a special dinner or as part of a Chinese-Indonesian feast!